IMPOSSIBLE POSSIBILITIES

LOUIS PAUWELS *and* JACQUES BERGIER

Are there intelligent beings on other planets—or in other galaxies? If there are, is there some way to communicate with them? Can man become immortal? Can an electronic brain learn to "think" for itself? Is there a fourth state of matter? Will ESP ever supplement—or supplant—speech as a means of communication?

Jacques Bergier and Louis Pauwels, authors of the highly acclaimed *The Morning of the Magicians,* have once again delved into the "outer limits" of scientific research. Working from the basic premise that the province of science is limited only by the human imagination and technological ingenuity, they shatter our conventional notions of what is really "impossible" from a scientific standpoint. "Impossible possibilities," they tell us, are the objects of some of the most intensive and dramatic research in the history of science.

The fascination of this book is matched only by its timeliness. Nearly every week newspaper headlines prove Pauwels and Bergier's contention that yesterday's "impossible possibilities" are tomorrow's realities.

IMPOSSIBLE POSSIBILITIES

BY THE SAME AUTHORS

The Morning of the Magicians

IMPOSSIBLE

LOUIS PAUWELS *and* JACQUES BERGIER

TRANSLATED BY ANDREW WHITE

POSSIBILITIES

𝔖𝔇 STEIN AND DAY/*Publishers*/New York

First published in the United States of America by Stein and Day, 1971
First published in Germany under the title
Der Planet der unmöglichen Möglichkeiten.
Copyright © 1968 by Scherz Verlag, Bern und München
Translation copyright © 1971 by Stein and Day, Incorporated
Library of Congress Catalog Card No. 75-151231
All rights reserved
Published simultaneously in Canada by Saunders of Toronto, Ltd.
Designed by David Miller
Manufactured in the United States of America
Stein and Day/*Publishers*/7 East 48 Street, New York, N. Y. 10017
ISBN 0-8128-1389-8

Contents

IMPOSSIBLE POSSIBILITIES

Prologue: A Few Thoughts

I have always known that the man who leaves his fatherland will be sick of nostalgia. Now I know that the man who leaves this earth will be prey to a similar malady, but I do not know how to name this affliction.

—German Titov

At the time when Jacques Bergier and I published the book *The Morning of the Magicians* we did not expect the work to find such a large public. The impact of the book, we thought, would be more one of depth than one of numbers—hopefully shaking its readers to the very core. We simply could not imagine that it would attract the general public.

The publication of the book was preceded by many years of careful research over a broad spectrum of knowledge: physics, biology, history, mysticism, literature, and more. Our aim was to reconcile to a certain extent ancient thinking based on the occult and on magic with the thought of our own time. The past and the future were viewed from the perspective of a method we called in that book "the fantastic;" the book ended with a prognosis for the future of mankind.

I have never stopped asking myself the three questions that have always moved the mind of man: Where do we come from? What are we? Where are we going? In *The Morning of the Magicians* we raised these questions once again, but this time with a contemporary slant, in an almost barbaric fashion, in the manner of hard-pressed men defending themselves with every weapon available to them, from the spear to the rocket, from the magical incantation to the mathematical equation.

We are living in a time when the question marks have grown to such gigantic proportions that they stretch way beyond our planet. The basic questions of mankind have regained their primeval meaning. In my view the time has come to move from Stendhal's ''Almighty God, why am I I?'' to ''Almighty God, why are we?'' In a world dominated by masses, by worldwide projects and cosmic myths, in a world turning out to be quite different from anything previously surmised, in which man senses significant change in himself, in such a world reliance on subjective psychology in the end undermines all psychology.

Undoubtedly the transition from the individual to the collective (and correspondingly from the psychological to the metaphysical) is painful for those of the privileged classes, and it is understandable that literature based upon glorification of the individual and concerned with the search for personal happiness is slow to take account of the change. In a letter to Constance Malleson, Bertrand Russell wrote the following magnificent lines:

> Before I die I must still find a way to express all that is essential within me and which I have still not been able to express, something that is neither love nor hate, neither pity nor scorn, but rather the warm breath of life itself wafting over us from afar, carrying with it into the life of mortal men the immeasurable, frightening, awe-inspiring and merciless might of non-human things.

Most literary works in France today are reminiscent of the worthless jottings scribbled down with stubborn and absurd care by sleepy convention participants listening to a wearisome lecture. As the fate of the individual becomes more and more bound up with the fate of mankind as a whole, and as, on the carpet of knowledge, the individual disciplines are twined together to provide an overall pattern, the writer slinks off sulking into his corner, there, as though in some bad daydream, to thread out labyrinthine literary puzzles, his horizon narrowing all the while. Balzac presented Paris or provincial France; in his work one loved according to part of the city one inhabited, with the sixteenth arrondissement as the favorite. This type of literature, the literature of individualization, is beginning to give off a smell of mold, while at the same time our entire planet is being aired by a fresh and seed-bearing wind, while the true story of today is one that moves in the realm of ideas, of technology, of social problems, and of mass psychology, while the individual consciousness is going through a painful process of expansion as it instinctively attunes to a new planetarian, cosmic consciousness.

As early as the nineteenth century the lamentable Maurice de Guérin, tossed between the bloated egotism of self-satisfaction and the indefinable presentiment of higher truths, gave voice to words that would well come from the lips of those contemporaries of ours who so squander their talent:

Dear God, how we complain about our isolation! I, too, was obsessed with this madness for a long time. In those days I lived wrongly, quite wrongly; the relationships I had fostered between the creatures of the earth and the innermost recesses of my being were false, and in consequence I suffered grievously, nature refusing to disclose to me the rich treasure of her joys and excluding me from her most intimate circle. I despaired, feeling deeply lonely; for me the earth was a worse place than an abandoned, totally barren desert island in the middle of a savage ocean. A frightening silence surrounded me. How nonsensical that was! The man who can attune himself to the universal harmony, whose soul can receive the signals of that harmony, that man knows no isolation.

Once the fateful turbulence tossing us about has subsided, and after all upheavals, the paucity of the space accorded to these events in our literature will be noticed with considerable astonishment. Literature is out of touch not only with the great political and military events of our time but also with the powerful undercurrent of deep disturbance that formed the basis of these events, cracking open the world to vistas of broader perspective. "There is nothing more beautiful on earth than to understand what is going on under the shadow of swords," Kipling wrote. But this thought never seems to enter the heads of those who stand on the sidelines of the mighty battles of our time, those contemporary authors who bore us with isolated, false data instead of joining together to tell the truth of history. Reading today's fiction engenders sentiments similar to those felt by a modern Chinese faced with a tea-blossom poem written by a literatus of the 1930s: final, idyllic hallucinations of an expiring world.

But who are we to allow ourselves so critical and reproachful a tone? We have no philosophy to teach, no school to found, no wisdom to propound. We are seekers, nothing more. The bounds and boundaries of our search can be stated: everything is a part of our terrain that nourishes in us the consciousness that we are not only contemporaries of our own time but also, in this stormy epoch of increasingly accelerated change, contemporaries of the future. For the most part literature bases itself on the assumption that man does not change, or rather on the belief that in spite of all modifications, the basic structures, the mechanism of the brain, the biological functions, and the deepest psychic states—everything, in other words, that constitutes *Homo sapiens,* in the form we have traditionally come to know him—do not change. The so-called literature of commitment shakes this belief just as little as so-called bourgeois literature.

In Bourget just as in Zola, in Montherlant just as in Sartre, man is always the same *Homo sapiens,* even if in different situations. Our opinion is that this perspective on man is too limited, although it doubtless made sense at a certain stage in the historical evolution of mankind. It is a perspective that does not do justice to the facts of life either of earlier cultures founded on belief in magic or of coming civilizations built upon technology. Floods of new knowledge about the far past and about the near future force us to the admission—if only as a hypothesis—that man cannot be understood by traditional formulas, that his intelligence and capacities are perhaps of a different nature than commonly assumed. It is not within our remotest intentions to give publicity to some pseudoscientific hocus-pocus of the sort paraded by money-minded charlatans trying to take advantage of the latest fads. But work in theoretical physics as well as in the physiology of the brain is making evident the possibility of hitherto unsuspected states of consciousness. Progressive sociologists have come to the realization that the changes taking place in the world today will also change man, that man will begin to see himself and the world with new eyes, that his destiny will take a new turn. Through the work of Teilhard de Chardin and C. S. Lewis, new, revolutionary concepts have been introduced even into the bulwark of Christian theology. We believe that both the literature of the left and the literature of the right are oriented toward the past insofar as they attempt to corral a broader-based, more fantastic human reality within the bounds of the traditional *Homo sapiens.* And for that reason they are outside the boundaries of our territory, in which the future is the prime focus.

"In the context of cosmic values—and this is the lesson of modern physics—only the fantastic has a chance of being true," wrote Teilhard de Chardin. J. Robert Oppenheimer said: "We learn how great the strangeness of the world is." And J. B. S. Haldane: "Reality is not only more fantastic than we think but also much more fantastic than anything we can imagine." In our view, the fantastic must be an ingredient of true modern realism, in all areas, the cosmic, the psychological, the historical, or the sociological. But what is the "fantastic"?

For most "educated" men the fantastic is a deformation of natural laws, the impossible become visible. Like the unusual and the bizarre it is one aspect of the picturesque. Nevertheless we believe that working with the picturesque is a waste of time, a bourgeois undertaking. For us the fantastic is not the result of a deformation but rather a manifestation of natural laws, the outcome of contact with reality experienced pure and direct without the soiling disfigurement that occurs when it passes through the filter of our ancient or modern prejudices.

Like all other cultures, our own is a conspiracy. a bevy of petty divinities who derive their power solely from our unprotesting acquiescence and constantly deflect our gaze away from the fantastic aspect of reality. The conspiracy causes us to renounce of our own free will the realization that there is another world within the world inhabited by us, another man inside the man known to us. It is imperative for us to break out of this pact, to leave the circle of conspirators. The only way to achieve this is to use differently the knowledge available to us, to establish fresh connections between the various branches of knowledge, to look at the facts of life with eyes cleared of the hypnosis of traditional values—in short, to conduct ourselves in the realm of the intellect like intelligent beings who came from elsewhere with the sole aim of seeking revelation. If we do behave in this way, the fantastic will always reveal itself to us simultaneously with the real.

This attitude has been adopted recently by our friends: young mathematicians, physicists, and biologists. One of them, the nuclear physicist Charles-Noel Martin, wrote to us:

Science is not by any means only that which the tradition of the nineteenth century would have us believe it to be, but is rather everything which our intelligences allow us to imagine both within us and in the world around us; the unusual, moreover, may not be either disregarded or underestimated, because we can neither say nor predict what the knowledge of later times will consist of. It may indeed be based upon concepts which we today ignore, but which our successors will recognize for their true significance in understanding mortal man and the manifestations of the phenomenal world at their new stage of scientific discovery.

Our sole aim is to approach all disciplines of knowledge with this open-minded attitude, especially the disciplines oriented to the study of man: psychology, archaeology, sociology, history, and so on. The journey takes us into a world that is just as wonderful, confusing, and strange as the world of the biologist, the physicist, the astronomer, or the mathematician. Everything hangs together. Proceeding along these lines we may stumble across a number of daring hypotheses and wondrous and unusual facts; the discovery of a few new truths topples a tower of legends and dreams. Every method has its disadvantages, some dubious results along with valuable new insights. But in our estimation the essential thing is the underlying intention of expanding man's view of his world, the inspiration we derive from the richness of this world, and our faith in its destiny. Those were the three factors that brought about the Renaissance.

But it is not just our literature that has failed to keep up with the ever-increasing pace of growth in human knowledge, with the restructuring of human society across the entire planet, and with the changes in the consciousness of man. It would be madness to find fault only with literature—a baroque embellishment in this age of space exploration. Looking around us we see on all sides spiritual currents flowing together to threaten and question the traditional image of man and the world. Every day piles of books arrive at our desks documenting the realization that a new culture is taking the place of the so-called modern culture. A science fiction novel from Soviet Russia takes up the theme of the "mutant" or of contact with an intelligent being from another planet. In Great Britain J. B. Priestley recently published a novel entitled *Saturn above the Water,* far bolder in concept than *The Morning of the Magicians.* In Germany Ceram, who had devoted his life to the interpretation of the past, suddenly changed the direction of his interests and published a book under his real name, Kurt Marek, called *Provocative Observations* in which, in the name of the near future, he objects to the fossilized forms of our culture. Many such examples could be cited, and we intend to do so in our periodical, *Planète*. The interest of the general public has not yet been awakened, and the new insights are the property of just a few people who are apt to be written off by others as eccentrics. But now we know how revolutions come about, we know that a complex organization with multiple branches can exist underground while the general belief is that the revolution consists of a few scattered individuals.

We do not of course have any intention of rejecting out of hand our heritage of humanistic culture in its entirety. It may no longer be attuned to phenomenal reality, but we still need it in order to answer certain questions that can only be answered with the aid of clear rationality and unconditional respect for the miracle of human life. At every period in our history these questions have been as numerous as they were urgent, and we should beware of disregarding them. If we were to do so, then in our effort to take a giant leap across humanism we would be leaving the solving of present-day problems in the hands of a non-culture. You cannot have geniuses in the laboratories and barbarians in the first-aid stations. The real concern must be to distinguish between problems completely different in their essentials. Even to perceive the problems we are talking about, let alone to solve them, requires an intellectual frame of mind not at all provided for in the heritage of our established cultural traditions. How can we assimilate a world-view that takes account of the revelations of the fantastic opened up by the new insights in the natural sciences? How can we grasp the future of mankind, its mass-population problems, and its planet-wide restructuring? How can the inner world of man be linked with a reality which lies outside him and which, as we know today, extends into infinity? There is nothing to prepare us for these powerful questions, and nothing even to help us ask them. Oppenheimer writes:

Today we are living in a world in which poets, historians, and philosophers declare with pride that they would not even remotely consider the possibility of studying anything which had to do with the natural sciences; for them science is at the other end of a tunnel far too long for a man of intelligence even to poke his head inside. Our philosophy—insofar as we have one at all—is therefore plainly anachronistic and totally out of step with our times.

On the other hand, it is of course true that too many scientists are not exactly hospitable to laymen. Only a few of them would share Dr. Burton's opinion that "it is not doing science a favor to discourage the interested layman." That particular difficulty can, however, be easily overcome. Not that we would presume to offer a new philosophy. We simply wish to send out a number of seekers in all directions, to raise new questions, and to keep their minds open to new answers. There is an old proverb that says: "The man who puts many questions often seems stupid, but the man who puts no questions stays stupid all his life."

In many areas of human knowledge and creation our general philosophy of life either fails us or turns out to be inadequate. These are the areas we want to probe and investigate in an attempt to correct our view of them and understand them. That can be done by studying certain aspects of zoology, biology, archaeology, psychology, mathematics, history, or the arts. There is no single front-line of attack but rather, as in all revolutions, numerous theaters of battle.

We seek to play a revolutionary role as witnesses of an underground movement to work out new forms of behavior and thought. We want to seek in history links with the world of tomorrow.

—Louis Pauwels

A Second Renaissance

That evening, as we were conversing through cigar-smoke at our flat in Baker Street, Sherlock Holmes gave voice to his opinion: "This is a case in which we were obliged to advance through deductions from the effects to the causes."

—Sir Arthur Conan Doyle

I do not believe in a spontaneous flowering of genius. Instead I am convinced that in the history of mankind there are moments of quite special significance. The image of the genius as lonely, as an elect suddenly struck with the lightning flash of revelation and instantly able to illuminate the gaping masses, is in my opinion false. A photograph of a trapeze artist in action would hardly give rise to the claim that the man was actually in flight, or hanging in the air at will. For a moment, it is true, he is like a bird, but the fact remains that gravity pulls him inexorably back down to earth. The same is true of the genius.

The poet Pierre de Ronsard (1524–1585) excelled in expressing the enchantment of nature, happiness at being alive, and the confusions of love. But he was able to do so only because a powerful turbulence was shaking our planet to its very foundations and a new spiritual climate was spreading, with the effect that man discovered new dimensions of human existence and new aspects of love. The Renaissance, which transformed Asia, extinguished Egypt, re-formed the West, caused the Church to tremble, rejuvenated antiquity, and paved the way for a future in which we still live, created upon Ronsard's flute a charming, well-turned, serene, heart-warming melody of blossoming freedom and retiring youthfulness—a sunrise serenade as happy music to accompany a pleasant life. That such a turbulence could evoke such human melodies—that is the miracle of poetry.

THE FIFTH CARAVEL AND THE FIRST ASTRONAUT

At the time when Ronsard was born in the peaceful, sun-filled Vendômois our planet was in the process of being transformed; men were discovering a new reality. The world of the Middle Ages had come to the end of its narrow track. I do not want to perpetuate in any way the old cliché that the period of the Middle Ages represents an epoch of obscurantism and ignorance in the history of mankind; indeed, recent discoveries about poetic and scientific developments in alchemy, analyses of the writings of Roger Bacon, Basilius Valentinus, and others, testify to the fact that there were bold minds at work in those days, tireless researchers, our predecessors, men of genius. Yet the structures of medieval society were ossified; scholasticism ruled everywhere and prevented much genuine progress in the world of knowledge.

In the Middle Ages the world was narrowly confined and surrounded by terrors and miracles. The sweeping horizons of antiquity had been strongly circumscribed; the gaze of man was directed toward heaven, toward God. The map of the world consisted to a large extent of blank areas thought to be the domains of demons and legendary monsters. In the thirteenth century, when Marco Polo brought news of China, which he called Cathay, to his contemporaries, nobody realized that the country in question was the same spoken of by Ptolemaeus under the name of Serica, and the Cathay described in *The Book of Miracles* was annexed on a mythical map to those far-off regions lumped together under the name "India." The West had lost its knowledge of Asia, and to all intents and purposes was ignorant of the great world of antiquity.

During the course of the fifteenth century the portals were suddenly opened once again. Henry the Navigator, the Portuguese *infant,* sent out expeditions that rediscovered Africa. The black continent, which had been penetrated by Muslims while Europeans had remained ignorant of its existence, suddenly re-emerged as part of the European world-view. Shortly afterward Bartholomeu Diaz rounded the Cape of Good Hope, thereby opening the sea route to India. Vasco da Gama rediscovered the Indian Ocean for European vessels, which had not been seen there for a thousand years. In the meantime Christopher Columbus, trying in the West to find the sea route to China and Japan, landed in Guanahani and Cuba, later discovering a new continent at the mouth of the Orinoco, although Amerigo Vespucci, at the beginning of the sixteenth century, was the first to properly recognize this discovery for what it was. In 1513 Pedro Cabral reached Brazil. High on a peak in the Central American mountains Vasco Núñez de Balboa gazed for the first time on the Pacific Ocean. All of a sudden the world was showing itself to men in its full greatness and multiplicity. These developments may be compared with the discovery in our time of the infinity of space—a new dimension. Vasco da Gama dared a voyage around the world. Only one of his five caravels succeeded in getting back to the home port of Seville. His journey was the most important event in the history of mankind until the first astronaut circled the earth.

THE FIRST FAREWELL FROM THE ORIENT

During the thirty years before the birth of Ronsard the three hundred ships that made up Portugal's fleets gave new contours to the globe. They sailed to Africa and Asia, anchored in Indian and Chinese harbors, transplanted the economic center of the earth to the European Atlantic coast, brought about the decline of the Mediterranean countries, and transformed the destiny of the Christian West. But while the trade routes were opening up, a spiritual exchange that had previously existed was breaking down. This development is clearly documented by Jacques Pirenne in his comprehensive study *The Great Currents of Universal History*. Alchemistic thinking, very much alive although underground throughout the Middle Ages, was intimately bound up with the intellectual life and scientific work of the Arabs, hence with Oriental and antique traditions. It should not be forgotten that the West had been under strong influence from the Orient ever since the eleventh century; contact between mysterious Asia and Europe had also transmitted to Westerners a certain sophistication, a fondness for luxury and for sensual pleasures, an inclination toward the fantastic and toward abandoned enjoyment.

However, while the Spanish and Portuguese set out to conquer the high seas, thereby gaining a huge lead over the French and English, who were weakened by the Hundred Years' War, the Turks were attempting to build up a new Roman Empire and were occupying the Byzantine territories one by one. Their military dictatorship completely suppressed the Arab culture. Constantinople had been a hub of traffic between East and West, and the culture of Córdoba, in which Hellenistic, Persian, and Western elements were intermingled, had been one of the high points of intellectual history. The Turkish annexation of Constantinople in 1453 closed off the communication that had united two great cultures through four centuries. Scholars and sages died; libraries containing collections of priceless worth went up in the flames. From that moment on the West never again had direct contact with a certain form of dreaminess and meditation, with a kind of mathematical and metaphysical knowledge, with a world of mysticism and poetry, in which sensuous aesthetics and the strictest asceticism had existed side by side.

As soon as the West had won physical control over the oceans, communication with the spiritual East stopped; the Orient sank into a deep slumber, awaiting the coming of its Prince to give the awakening kiss. Europe, caught in the grip of revolutionary changes in class structure, and suddenly rich, girded itself to colonize the earth. Although there were powerful increases in its cunning and political might, its virtues and its higher, purely spiritual knowledge were diminishing. Europe progressed in the direction of Materialism and Rationalism, which at first certainly opened up undreamed-of possibilities, but which later plunged the continent into the danger of self-destruction, a danger we in our time have escaped by the narrowest hair's breadth. The present is once again surrounded by immense turbulences; as at the beginning of the sixteenth century, the human spirit is once more trembling at its roots.

LOST SOURCES

During the Renaissance the sun rose in the West for the first time in the history of our planet. Asia was defeated by the brutal expansion of Turkish might and by the Portuguese conquests at sea. Cut off in the Mediterranean by the Turks and in the Indian Ocean by the Portuguese, Asia encapsulated itself, withdrawing into its own riches and mysteries. Possibilities for an exchange of ideas were all but eliminated. The earth was split into two worlds. The Far East, oriented exclusively around China, soon sealed itself completely from the West; Asia, which was Muslim, was divided into three parts: the Ottoman Empire, slowly suffocating under a repressive military rule; the Persian Empire, in which a radical nationalism was worshipped; and the feudal empire in India, ruled by a Turkish military aristocracy. Egypt, once a cradle of culture, a citadel of wisdom and spiritual life, lost all its significance after the destruction of Alexandria.

The West prospered, all routes stood open to the conquerors from the Atlantic coastlands. But the dissemination of Western power went hand in hand with a growing isolation. The price for the formation of modern consciousness was the break with an ancient cultural and spiritual heritage. The vertical movement of the spirit—the descent of truth from heaven to earth and the ascension into heaven of truth made flesh—fundamental not only to the Christian culture of the Middle Ages but also to Arab, Indian, Chinese, and Egyptian culture, was replaced in the West by a horizontal movement, an expansion of earthbound human possibilities, a humanistic imperialism. It spelled the end of feudal Christianity, an end explained at least in part by the break with the spirituality of the East. The wealth of the Church declined, and religion became, to a certain extent, secularized. It was as though Christianity had been loosed from its origins, as though its most ancient wells had run dry.

To be sure, the sixteenth century was still a Christian century—mention need only be made of the religious wars. But to quote Léopold Sédar Senghor: ''For the first time a distinction is made between the sacred and the profane.'' Even belief now tried to base itself on reason.

The voice of seventeenth-century formalism, parading a pompous, intellectual religiosity, was already to be heard.

RETURN TO THE SOURCES

While Europe was undergoing such change its eyes were blinkered against the reality of anything not part of an intellectual life centered on reason, pragmatism, and the lust for power. In the seventeenth and eighteenth centuries no one thought of ascribing greatness of any kind to the spirit or soul of the East. The Islamic world was portrayed in love stories from *A Thousand and One Nights,* India through Rameau's gallantries on stage. For three centuries the humanistic West believed itself to represent the ultimate stage of evolution, the uncontested ruler of the entire earth, while non-Europeans, it was assumed, remained stuck at some primitive spiritual level.

The exchange of ideas between West and East began again only in the second half of the nineteenth century. Through Schopenhauer and Nietzsche the East sent mighty underground shockwaves of uneasiness across the all too self-confident West. At the beginning of the twentieth century René Guénon and his disciples turned back to traditionalist thinking and resorted once more to the sources of spiritual religiosity. Last but not least, science challenged the foundations of knowledge and revelation taken as valid since the sixteenth century, while at the same time China, Africa, India, and the Islamic world awoke from their slumber and, with the aid of Western weaponry, won themselves a place in the political arena of the planet.

THE REDISCOVERY OF FREEDOM

The Hundred Years' War led to a dissolution of feudal structures. Power passed from the knights, feudal princes, and clergy to the meritocracy and laymen, who replaced divine right with human right. Freedom, or at least a breath of it, was able to waft in through the larger meshes of these new social textures. The growing economic significance of the cities improved the status of the middle class. Trade and commerce flourished, and fresh riches were shipped into the harbors of Europe.

All this progress led to a liberalization of the life of the mind: man gained new significance as an individual; reason was his guide and freedom his right. Research to uncover the realities of his immediate environment went hand in hand with geographical discoveries. Thanks to the compass, ships could sail all oceans; the invention of the printing press made the dissemination of an abundance of new ideas possible. The spirit of discovery, rejuvenated, made astonishing headway in a world in which medieval miracles existed alongside the wonders of scientific experiments. Leonardo da Vinci, a Jules Verne of his time, designed a diving suit, a submarine, an airplane, and was able to perceive, in general terms, the principle of gravity. Copernicus announced the world was round, and argued that our planet revolved around the sun. Mercator (Gerhard Kremer) laid the groundwork for scientific geography. Andreas Vesalius founded modern anatomy, Ambroise Paré opened new pathways for surgical research, and Agricola (Georg Bauer) laid the foundation for geological study. Knowledge built upon deduction replaced knowledge based upon revelation, doubt shattered authority, reason over faith.

The evolution of society to a concept of individual right and the major discoveries that provided the West with self-confidence coincided with a return to the spiritual world of antiquity. For seven centuries the connection with this world had been broken. What man found now was not really new, merely forgotten.

THE YOUTHFULNESS OF THE ANCIENTS

The Renaissance had its origins in Italy. Petrarch revived the Roman epic, Boccaccio reintroduced the study of Greek. In 1440 Plethon founded a Platonic academy in Florence. After the fall of Constantinople numerous scholars came to the West bringing priceless manuscripts they had managed to save. Massilio Filino started the scientific study of the Greek language, while Pico della Mirandola made the study of Hebrew fashionable. Christopher Columbus copied out twice the second-act chorus from Sophocles' *Medea,* in which the poet writes of a world destined for discovery by later centuries. In Aristotle's *De Caelo* he found the statement that the earth was round.

At the time of Descartes' birth many men of the Renaissance already knew Aristotle's dictum: "The man who wishes to educate himself must first know how to doubt, because the doubting mind can get to the truth.'' They already knew that Democritus allowed the validity only of those experiments at which he had himself been present, the results of which he had verified with the imprint of his signet ring. Long before Newton Pythagoras had established the law that when two bodies attract each other the force in effect is in inverse proportion to the square of the distance. Thales had described the Milky Way, Lucretius had put forth the idea of infinite space filled by countless worlds, Plutarch had anticipated the laws of gravity. Galileo and Newton stress how much they owed to the thinkers of antiquity. In the preface to his principal opus Copernicus writes that the idea of the earth being in movement came to him while he was reading the authors of antiquity.

But the Renaissance was far more than a return to Greco-Roman literature and aesthetics. Modern modes of thought, already present in essence in the writings of the researchers of antiquity, blossomed during the favorable climate of the sixteenth century, and we are still reaping its astonishing fruits today. Even nuclear physics seems to be anticipated in antiquity. In his *Epistle on Miracles* Roger Bacon writes: "In accordance with the few examples which I have granted to nature and art, we can deduce several things from the one thing, the whole from its parts, and the general from the particular. In addition we have seen that it would be senseless to resort to magic for help: nature and science suffice us.''

Even in the Middle Ages this spirit of inquiry with origins in antiquity, oriented toward the future yet inspired by the ancients, had never really been completely extinguished. It may be assumed that both the spirit and the inspiration were kept alive during the entire Christian Middle Ages by alchemy. During the sixteenth century the works of alchemists, handwritten and printed, were in circulation, especially the writings of Basilius Valentinus, destined later to arouse the enthusiasm of Leibnitz: "I decided to study nature, to inquire into its secrets through its structures, and so to come to know that which after things eternal counts among the highest things of this earth.''

From 1540 in Germany and 1545 in France we may trace the development of groups which produced the freemasons. Around the same time the brotherhood of the Rosicrucians was founded, which brought together men interested in the past as well as the future. As is well known, freemasons and Rosicrucians played a decisive part in the French Revolution.

FRESH WIND IN THE SAILS

It was not long before the Renaissance spread from Italy to France. Ronsard, Antoine de Baïf, and Joachim du Bellay all studied with Dorat, who taught the literature of antiquity. No doubt they were attracted to these studies by their desire to renew French poetry, but their passionate search for new insights and their obsession for converting Greco-Roman subjects into verse actually stemmed from impulses going far beyond a purely literary interest. They were caught in a current sweeping Western man uncontrollably along. Their strivings in the literary sphere were part of a general turbulence, the force of which enabled them to achieve their aims.

The sense of inspiration they felt was almost unimaginable. Ronsard would persist with his studies until two or three in the morning, then awaken Baïf, who would get up, take over the candle, "and not let the chair get cold." Strict discipline was the password of these colloquiums, in which a new spirit was coaxed out of the texts of antiquity. In an excellent book on Ronsard André Berry writes:

Four o'clock was wake-up time. A student went through all the rooms to light the candles and shake up all those who were still lounging in bed. After morning prayers, at about five o'clock, the students went to the first classes, carrying a candle in one hand and bulky books under the other arm. Until ten o'clock, without interruption, they listened to the words of their teacher. At ten-thirty lunch was taken. After the meal the students relaxed while reading the works of Sophocles, Aristophanes, Euripides, and sometimes Virgil, Cicero, or Horace. At one o'clock classes began again, and lasted until five in the afternoon. After that the students had to read over, in their own copies of the works, quoted texts cited by the teacher. Next it was time for chapel and the evening mass. In winter bedtime was at eight o'clock, in summer at nine.

The wind of freedom blows away tiredness. Studying the wisdom of antiquity leads to knowledge about tomorrow, learning the songs of antique man is an attunement to the sound of tomorrow's voices. Ronsard called Dorat "the awakener of dead science."

TOWARD A NEW PLÉIADE

Striking similarities link our time to the Renaissance. In the sixteenth century men busied themselves without prejudices with the world of antiquity; today men research the distant past of mankind—and while perspectives on the future broaden, the past is illuminated as far back as possible. The spirit of discovery manifest in the most recent advances in archaeology, anthropology, and paleontology may be compared to the turbulence that drove the men of the Renaissance back to Greco-Roman sources. Today, alongside attempts to understand the most distant cultures and discover the first traces of mankind, man is trying to explore regions beyond the earth with the help of rockets. In addition to his attempts to open up the infinite spectrum of the universe man is trying to discover more about his origins. Just as our ancestors sensed the dissolution of the foundations of medieval spiritual life and of the cultural structures of the Christian Middle Ages, so we today sense that the foundations of humanistic culture have been shaken, and that the bulwarks of modern knowledge, of Cartesian thought, at its fullest bloom during the nineteenth century, are beginning to crumble. "Long ago," writes Oppenheimer, "we should have set ourselves the task of examining more intensively the nature of human intelligence and the relationship between man and the universe."

We want at the same time to learn from lost cultures and to establish communications with intelligent beings in the universe. We traverse the cosmos in search of a somewhere else, and we traverse our planet ·in search of our origins. In all areas of knowledge—natural sciences, psychology, sociology—we see the disintegration of the frontiers that until yesterday bounded our thought. We are moving toward a time of awakening and of wonders in which everything is possible, in which the mind will undergo a profound transformation and be ready to receive the great secrets of the creation. It is astonishing that this state of a completely unbounded imagination and a consciousness stretched to the uttermost, comparable to a certain extent with the state experienced by a Renaissance artist, does not inspire appropriate poetry and music, hymns to the glory of human existence, and that this mighty turbulence does not find harmonious expression in the words of our generation. But we are still at the beginning of the development. Our art and literature still belong to yesterday, just as the generation of Francis I belonged to the past and yet at the same time felt torn by the call of the future.

Let us wait and hope that our time of rebirth can bring forth a new Pléiade.

—Louis Pauwels

Three Windows on Infinity

Chance created distances. Only the mind can change everything.

—Beaumarchais

WE SEND SIGNALS TO THE STARS

The first man to suggest communicating with the possible inhabitants of other planets through light signals was the German mathematician Karl Friedrich Gauss (1777–1855); later the idea was taken up by the French poet and inventor Charles Cros. They proposed to light huge fires in Siberia or the Sahara arranged in a design representing a classical geometrical theorem, for instance, Pythagoras' law. Intelligent beings on other planets would then draw the conclusion that there were rational beings on earth and would answer through signals of their own. Their theory found strong support. At the beginning of the twentieth century a stout-hearted Frenchwoman went so far as to bequeath her fortune to the man successful in finding a way to communicate with the inhabitants of other planets. However, she wrote into her will that the legacy could not be paid out if the planet in question turned out to be Mars—because that was too easy! In the end the experiment was never carried out because it seemed too absurd. All the same, it inspired an attractive story from the Irish writer Lord Dunsany: using giant searchlights men set up a representation of Pythagoras' law in the Sahara desert. The inhabitants of Mars react by signaling at first the same configuration, but then they start shifting the lines to come up with a new shape, representing mathematical power. On earth, mankind understands what is meant: the Martians are stating in no uncertain terms that they want no communication.

A new invention, the laser beam, has renewed interest in this problem. The laser is an electronic instrument that generates sharply concentrated light rays of high energy. The idea for the laser is based on research by the French scientist Alfred Kastler; in 1958 the idea was taken up again by the Americans Charles H. Townes and Arthur L. Schawlow. The first laser was built in July 1960, by T. H. Maiman in the laboratories of the Hughes Aircraft Company. An artificial ruby, energized in a particular way, emits a ray brighter than sunlight. The light rays, concentrated in the crystal and transmitted as an intensive red beam of light, last for about one-half-thousandth of a second. The intensity of the beam is unimaginable. An area of less than one square centimeter emits light energy equal to 10,000 watts; the energy emitted by the sun over the same area is only 6 watts. Over a distance of three-fifths of a mile the light beam deviates at most one yard from its course. Using laser beams it would theoretically be possible to project onto the moon's surface a circle of light measuring three miles in diameter and visible from long distances away. And that would by no means exhaust the possibilities of the laser beam. A concentration of beams can increase the intensity up to 100 million watts per square centimeter!

And yet the invention is only in its very beginnings. In July 1961 the president of the Soviet Academy of Sciences declared that he could foresee building lasers strong enough to generate light signals visible from a distance of dozens of light-years. Signals of this strength could be perceived by possible inhabitants of the planets that revolve around stars like Tau Ceti and Epsilon Eridani. This invention is therefore the first window open today on other worlds.

THE SECOND WINDOW: RADIO ASTRONOMY

The second window on infinity is opened by electromagnetics. It was pried ajar for the first time by one of the greatest inventors of all time, Thomas Alva Edison. There is an eye-witness account of his idea. As his scientific advisor and collaborator he took on Prof. A. E. Kennelly, the first scientist to postulate the presence of ionized layers in the upper atmosphere. On November 2, 1890 (before the discovery of radioactivity, before the discovery of X-rays, before the first airplane), Professor Kennelly wrote to a colleague, Dr. Holden, director of the Lick Observatory in the United States, that he and Edison intended to try to pick up electromagnetic rays emitted by the sun; they were working on the assumption that these rays would be attracted by iron ore. The experiment was unsuccessful, because its basic premise was wrong; nonetheless Edison, father of electric light, may also be regarded as the founder of radio astronomy In 1894 his idea was taken up again by Sir Oliver Lodge. After that followed a period of thirty-eight years during which radio astronomy remained a province of science-fiction authors. But then came the breakthrough. A historical essay appeared in the December 1932 number of the famous American periodical *Proceedings of the Institute of Radio Engineers.* It was signed with the name Carl Jansky.

Jansky was a technologist in the employ of the Bell Radio Corporation; his job was to track down, with the aid of a rotating antenna, the origins of interferences in radio reception. Apart from the interferences created by electromagnetic storms, automobiles, and airplanes he picked up noises traceable to electromagnetic waves out of space. The waves were being transmitted neither by the sun nor by the earth. They came from a direction leading straight into the center of our Milky Way galaxy. The event marked the discovery of radio astronomy. An amateur radio enthusiast in America named Reber, interested in Jansky's researches, built a rotatable antenna in his garden, measuring 10 meters in diameter. Jansky was operating on the 15-meter frequency. Reber built a receiver which transmitted over 60-cm waves. Then he began to construct the first radio maps of the invisible heavens. He discovered the radio waves emitted by the sun and was able to establish that invisible sources of rays exist in the universe, especially in the constellations Cassiopeia, Swan, and Bull. He published the results of his research between 1940 and 1942, around the same time radar was invented. The Soviets, under the direction of I. S. Schklowsky, also began to turn their attention to radio astronomy. And so the second window in our earthly cell was opened once and for all. Now it was possible for man to pick up signals from heavenly bodies unimaginably distant from our own planet.

THE THIRD WINDOW: THE SECRET OF PONTECORVO

The third window is still closed but in the process of being opened. Research activities in this direction were reported during January 1961

in the Soviet Union. The periodical *Soviet Studies* published the
following unusual text:

Is it true that man has hit upon a way to discover the "other world"? That
man can look at the sun through the earth? A report submitted to the
Cosmological Committee of the Astronomical Advisory Board in the Soviet
Academy of Sciences was devoted to this question and others all but
incredible.

We were able to consult the author of the report, Professor Bruno
Pontecorvo, corresponding member of the Soviet Academy of Sciences: he
talked to us about the incredible properties of the neutron, an elemental
particle that promises to become an important aid in research into the secrets
of the cosmos.

But in what respects can neutrons be useful in helping us to carry
out research into the secrets of the cosmos?

Until the present time information about space has come to us
exclusively via electromagnetic waves (light and radio waves), which
enlightened us only about the surface of stars. But massive
concentrations of neutron rays will enable us to garner insights about
the innermost recesses of these stars. For stars—at least those in which
atom fusions occur in the same manner as in our sun—generate
neutrons in huge masses.

It is still not possible to receive radiograms from the heart of far-off
constellations via neutrons, because we do not yet possess instruments
sensitive enough to register the neutrons as they bounce off.

The sun, however, is another matter. Every second an unimaginable
number of neutrons beamed out from the sun penetrate every square
yard of the earth's surface. It is an extremely difficult operation to
"capture" such a flood of neutrons, but it is possible. The time is
presumably not far off when man will be able to study the atomic
processes that go on behind the chromosphere and photosphere of the
sun. Man will then be able to look right into the solar "atomic reactor"
and establish the exact nature of solar energy.

The prospects for neutron astronomy are even more exciting when
the more distant future is contemplated.

Every elemental particle has its antipode, alike in appearance but
opposite in electric charge. The antipode of the negative electron is,
for instance, the positive positron. ("Charge" in this context should

not be understood merely as electrical charge.) The neutron has its antipode too, the anti-neutron, which can be distinguished from the neutron by the manner in which it spins: the neutron spins from right to left, the anti-neutron from left to right. Theoretically it is possible that there exist in space constellations, planets, and galaxies constructed of anti-matter: an "antipode world."

Until now there has been no way of establishing whether or not such an antipode world exists in fact. Yet verification of the hypothesis would have enormously significant implications for physicists and astronomers. Certainty on this point would permit answers to many questions about the origins of the galaxies.

Neutron astronomy opens up, theoretically, the possibility of documenting the existence of an antipode world in space. The uncharged elemental particles emitted by the sun are for the most part neutrons. Anti-neutrons are hardly in evidence. An antipode sun would on the other hand emit for the most part anti-neutrons into space. Establishment of the relationship between neutrons and anti-neutrons in the rays beamed out from the constellations would tell us whether we are dealing with a heavenly body of the same kind as our sun, or whether it is an antipode.

DECISIVE REASONS FOR PACIFISM

We have, therefore, three windows open upon infinity. But how can we lean out to take a look? Will we be able to explore the cosmos free of hindrance? No. Our own activities create obstacles: Astronomy, working with optic instruments, is immensely hampered by air pollution. Radio astronomy is on the verge of almost total paralysis, since the giant radio telescopes, highly sensitive parabola antennas, pick up every single electromagnetic wave. They receive radio and television transmitters, radar stations, and in addition electric motors, electric razors, toys run by electricity, and so on.

In the United States radio telescopes have been set up hundreds of miles away from the nearest human settlement. Research workers and technicians employed there have to go to work by bicycle. The use of electric razors is forbidden. And yet even these precautions are not enough, for there are artificial satellites to reckon with, signals reflected from meteors, difficulties in reception. A still greater threat for radio astronomers is the American-Soviet project of building in the atmosphere a girdle of tin foil that surrounds the earth and reflects all electromagnetic waves. During World War II radar installations were put out of action with such foil. This project would, it is true, facilitate worldwide radio and telephone communications; but at the same time it would close mankind off from the stars forever, since the waves coming in from space would strike the outer side of the girdle and be bounced back.

Last but not least, radio astronomers are also protesting atomic blasts executed at great heights, since such explosions release highly disturbing ionized layers in the atmosphere.

Radio astronomy is an extraordinarily important science. It opens up to us the possibility of communicating with intelligent beings in the cosmos, and provides us with information of great significance about the universe.

Mankind would be inexpressibly foolish if, at the very moment when space flights have begun, it were to close again one of the three windows on infinity and voluntarily shut itself off within the vastness of space.

The third form of astronomy, neutron astronomy, has as yet no concrete existence. The day it starts we may be able to localize all sources of atomic energy in the bowels of the earth itself. We will be able to establish where hydrogen, the isotope necessary for the manufacture of hydrogen bombs, is stored. A few neutron telescopes under the supervision of an international control commission would be enough to bring about controlled disarmament.

Keeping open the three windows depends more upon the evolution of mankind than upon the evolution of science in the narrow sense. Provision would have to be made at an international level to reserve certain areas on the earth for observatories, radio telescopes, and neutron observation stations. Transmissions over the wavelength on which the second window is open would have to be forbidden by international law. The continued contamination of the atmosphere by atomic tests would have to be stopped. The fundamental interests of mankind coincide with the most advanced scientific interests.

At this point many might well ask, Why? Hasn't mankind got on all right up to now without communication with intelligences beyond the earth? Is there really any sense in trying to set up such a communication?

When Faraday was asked, "What use is electricity?" he answered, "What use is a newborn child?"

—Jacques Bergier

New Hypotheses
of Modern Astronomy

A THICKET OF THEORIES

Ever since man raised his eyes the grandeur of the skies has fascinated him. Many centuries were necessary, during which instruments became more and more sophisticated, before he was in a position to perceive the texture of the canopy of heaven. When he could at last see it, he still could not understand how it had been put together. At the moment when the scientist believes he has achieved some certainty about the structure of the cosmos, one signal from space topples his theories. During the past decade alone there have been a number of peaceful upsets of this kind.

The cosmos that is beginning to deliver up some of its secrets to us today is fundamentally different from the universe man believed he knew before the space age began.

Today comets—mist-encircled masses of which the path but not the origin is known—are regarded as relatively young heavenly bodies; many are scarcely ten thousand years old and are presumed to have been hurled into space by volcanic eruptions of giant stars. The constellation of Saturn is also thought to be of recent date, still unstable and only in the first stages of organization. New heavenly bodies come into being in our own constellation too, just as new galaxies—even groups of galaxies—form themselves.

Between the galaxies unknown sources of energy are at work that have nothing to do with gravity. In general, the universe is no longer looked upon today as a gigantic, stationary whole; the contemporary belief is that it is in the process of constant change. And yet it seems to have existed since all eternity and to have no spatial limits.

The expansion of the universe and the sweep of the galaxies into infinity (a theory put forward in 1921 by Abbé Georges Édouard Lemaître) is thought today to be a local phenomenon limited to the range of the observation instruments available at the time: perception of a contraction taking place in other regions of the cosmos. Similarly, it can no longer be supposed that the universe is composed of the same matter everywhere. The probability is that certain areas of the universe are constructed out of anti-matter, while in other parts proto-matter is the substance: neither matter nor anti-matter but rather a neutral substance that separates at intervals to produce matter and anti-matter. Many regions of the cosmos are still in chaos, still in a kind of primitive state.

This world-view blurs the perspectives handed down to us, and cannot be allied to what we have been taught. And yet it is an inevitable consequence of the facts as observed in the most recent times. However, when the day comes that observatories in space are at our disposal, it will seem much less extraordinary.

A BILLION INHABITED PLANETS IN OUR MILKY WAY GALAXY?

It seems that the universe has bounds neither in time nor in space—a viewpoint held particularly by most Soviet astronomers. Beyond the metagalaxy, to which all known galaxies belong, there must be still more worlds.

The metagalaxy consists of hypergalaxies (groups of galaxies). Two "satellites" belong to our galaxy: the huge Magellan nebula, 38,000 parsec away from us (1 parsec=3.26 light-years), and the small Magellan nebula, 36,000 parsec from us. The Andromeda nebula is a system of five galaxies. Joining those galaxies that form a group is usually a "bridge" made up of stars. The groups of galaxies are, as it were, "balanced" on an axis consisting of stars. Such hypergalaxies can be unimaginably powerful: the constellation Virgo is made up of 3000 galaxies, "Berenice's Hair" of 10,000. Supergalaxies have a diameter of 30 to 40 parsec. The precise number of supergalaxies that makes up a metagalaxy is not known. And yet the metagalaxy we conceive of is merely a fraction of the infinite, boundless universe that has existed for billions of years and will exist for all eternity. In so gigantic a world, in part unknown and its known part infinitely complicated, the human mind has difficulty comprehending the overall order.

Since the universe is boundless, it can neither expand nor contract. Only the metagalaxy is expanding. It was probably formed about ten billion years ago by the explosion of a cloud of proto-matter, at which time, it is assumed, a metagalaxy of anti-matter also came into existence.

We are living in a part of the universe that is expanding; other parts are contracting. In the opinion of the Russian scientist G. I. Naan, this contraction in other areas of the universe is resulting in a reversal of time.

Many cosmologists—Thomas Gold, for instance—hold the view that life, like matter, is eternal, and is disseminated from solar system to solar system by living beings with the help of interstellar spaceships. This is a bold hypothesis, but most modern researchers who reject it are nevertheless ready to admit that highly developed forms of life, able to influence nature much more than we on earth can see, may have arisen in many parts of the universe. They believe that there are probably a billion inhabited planets in our Milky Way galaxy.

PROTO-MATTER OR THE ORIGIN OF THE STARS

These planets revolve of course around suns; they vary in age. The American astronomer Allan Sandage discovered that some planets where there is the possibility of life may be twenty-eight billion years old.

Our planet is assumed to be no more than four billion years old, with life on it only for approximately two billion years. If life on a twenty-eight-billion-year-old planet also began two billion years after its origin, then it has had twenty-six billion years to reach perfection—thirteen times the period of life on earth until now. What stage of evolution has life reached on these planets? Perhaps one day we shall know the answer, if ever we receive a visit from outer space. But this simple example shows that the question concerning the origin of the stars is of more than academic interest.

Traditional astronomy teaches that stars are formed by condensation of dustlike stellar material. The Soviet astronomer V. A. Ambartsumian takes a different view; in his opinion stars are formed from unimaginably thick proto-stars, formed not from matter or anti-matter but from proto-matter. This proto-matter explodes, causing the formation of a group of stars. The proto-matter is of tremendous density, corresponding approximately to that of the atom. The proto-stars emit no rays and cannot be perceived by telescope. But the consequences of their explosions are visible as newly formed stars encircled by nebulae. Ambartsumian has discovered such groups of stars, especially in the constellation of Perseus, where supernovae are in the process of formation. In other parts of the heavens too he has found mounds of stars less than 100,000 years old.

The Soviet astronomer does not claim to have found the one and only cause and the one imaginable process of star formation. He does not exclude the possibility that stars may be formed according to the classical formula—by a contraction of matter. Nevertheless he considers such formation to be an exceptional rather than typical case, since in his opinion stars are formed not gradually but suddenly, through a process triggered by an explosion. This theory is in harmony with the latest concept of the universe, according to which there is no such thing as a static cosmos or rigid universe, and never will be.

As is the case with the splitting of the uranium atom, it is possible that a galaxy might cause one or more smaller galaxies to come into being under the impact of forces completely unknown to us. Enormously powerful electromagnetic rays are released by such a split in the galaxy, and can be picked up by radio telescope. Such rays have been particularly noticeable in the constellations Swan and Perseus.

Unstable galaxies of this type appear bluish white in the telescope, because fragments are hurled with considerable force into space by the explosion. The possibility is there that an entire metagalaxy consists of the splinters of a gigantic star that has exploded. If this is the case, the expansion of the universe would indeed be a very localized phenomenon.

Our own metagalaxy would thus turn out to be nothing more than a backwater, a special case to be seen in the context of the universe as a whole, a universe unable either to expand or contract. In consequence, nothing observed upon our metagalaxy would permit conclusions about the universe as a whole. Space would thereby be cramped only in our metagalaxy.

It may be that we should abandon the idea of a self-contained universe contoured something like the earth's surface, despite the relative newness of the thought. Once again the indication is that we should be cautious of drawing analogies: what applies here does not necessarily apply in space; the atom is not a solar system in miniature; the universe not a four-dimensional copy of the earth's surface. It is not possible to circle the universe as Magellan sailed around the earth. Once again man's innate intellectual laziness has led to a view of the universe as a whole as a larger version of the world already known to him; whereas in reality the universe is and will remain for the most part unknown.

Even the unimaginable, infinitely vast universe is probably not the whole reality. Beyond it there must be at least a second universe, the world of anti-matter.

IS THERE AN ANTIPODE WORLD BEYOND THE WORLD?

Using giant atom smashers of the type that can be found at the European Atomic Research Center in Geneva, modern science has been able to generate anti-matter particles such as anti-protons, anti-neutrons, and so on. With the aid of these atom smashers, new particles are constantly being discovered. No scientist has as yet succeeded in constructing anti-matter out of these laboratory particles, but this process is theoretically possible. It may be surmised that worlds in collision long ago realized the task that man has not yet been able to achieve.

Famous scientists like Geoffrey Burbridge and Fred Hoyle are convinced that "somewhere" there exists an antipode world of anti-matter. It may well be that this world is situated beyond space and in another time. In such an event the unknown would be superimposed upon the known; a world of specters may be accompanying us constantly, or perhaps we are accompanying it. Burbridge and Hoyle believe that the two worlds come together in the vast Crab

Constellation, that matter and anti-matter collide there and destroy each other. It is a fact that this constellation emits rays of extraordinary energy, electromagnetic waves with an intensity of 10^{33} ergs per second, which corresponds to approximately 100 billion atom bombs of Hiroshima strength per second.

If calculations are based on the mass of energy observed to have been released, the conclusion can be arrived at mathematically that in this constellation there must be one anti-matter particle for every ten million matter particles. This part of the universe is like a giant oven in which worlds are burned.

It is possible that the galaxy Messier 87 consists wholly and completely of anti-matter. It transmits both visible light and radio waves in unusual quantities. One explanation might be the surmise that this galaxy is in fact an advance post of the anti-world constantly showered by normal matter.

Professor Maurice Goldhaber of the American atomic research institute in Brookhaven believes that the anti-matter antipode world came into being at the same time as our universe through an explosion of proto-matter. According to his theories the anti-world exists outside of space and in another time, but he considers it possible that there are other ways in which fragments of the antipode world get to us.

FROM PASCUAL JORDAN . . .

Many scientists, Pascual Jordan for instance, go even further. In their opinion there exist gigantic chains of parallel worlds in a fifth dimension of reality. From these parallel worlds not only matter and anti-matter atoms, but also planets, suns, and entire galaxies can enter into our universe. According to their theories, the constant transformation of matter into energy in the suns would be compensated for through the constant supply of new matter from other worlds.

Jordan goes so far as to believe it possible that the human mind has access to these other worlds and that certain parapsychological phenomena can be explained by this circumstance. He seems to be alone in holding this opinion, except for science fiction authors, who for half a century have been making use of the theory of the existence of parallel worlds—in some cases in a brilliant manner. Jordan has been decried as an occultist, because his parallel worlds bear a strong resemblance to the astral bodies of the theosophists and anthroposophists. But that is doing the scientist an injustice. His ideas might be highly original and out of the way, but they are scientifically based.

. . . TO EAVESDROPPING ON THE STARS

Over the last decade new methods of observation have led to radical transformations of the cosmogony. A major part of what is known today about the universe does not derive from traditional optic telescopes but from radio telescopes, with the help of which man is able to receive radio waves emanating in space.

These electromagnetic waves were discovered in the United States by Carl G. Jansky. In 1951 the American astronomer Walter Beade, using a 5-meter telescope atop Mount Palomar, was able to establish that such radio waves originate, among other areas, in the Swan constellation about 700 million light-years away. It has since been possible, thanks to huge radio telescopes in Cambridge, England, and Sydney, Australia, to fix the origins of several thousand such radio waves. In not one single case are the signals generated artificially: the high-frequency beams are so powerful in energy that their origins must be natural phenomena. The strength of the rays ranges from 10^{28} to 10^{34} kilowatts. That corresponds to 100,000 to 100 billion atom bombs of Hiroshima strength per second. If signals generated by intelligent beings were in fact to come to us from outer space, we would need hypersensitive instruments to be able to sift them out from the mass of naturally generated rays. The radio waves reaching us from the outer universe permit us to perceive the existence of objects beyond the boundaries of space-worlds perceivable through optical telescopes. But where do these radio waves originate?

MESSAGES FROM OUTER SPACE AND THE SECRET OF THE RADIO WAVES

The first hypothesis on the origin of the radio waves from outer space was put forward in 1940. It came from an American science-fiction author named Edward Elmer Smith. In his novel *The Guardians of the Milky Way* he posits the possibility of a collision between two Milky Way galaxies. For the inhabitants of the planets such a collision would not be dangerous, since it passes off too slowly. But the two galaxies in collision would give off gases which, acting upon each other, would cause a strong transmission of radio waves. Today the opinion is generally held that Smith's imaginative genius anticipated a phenomenon that does in fact exist and that may be observed in certain regions of the heavens.

This theory does not of course explain the origins of all radio waves. Nor does the surmise that the radio waves originate at the spots where our world and the antipode world of anti-matter collide provide sufficient explanation. There must be such spots, but they are very rare.

What other explanations are possible? In 1953 the Soviet radio astronomer I. S. Schklowsky put forward a new theory. It should be said at once that Schklowsky is a completely serious scholar and that his theory has obtained general recognition. In his view radio waves originate when electrons moving through space almost at the speed of light are trapped in the magnetic field of a galaxy. These electrons are presumably released from exploding stars and the formation of novae. If this theory is accurate, then many sources of radio waves are of relatively recent date—the source in the Swan constellation would be no older than 400,000 years.

Working on observations he had gathered at Yerkes Observatory in the United States, Geoffrey Burbridge arrived recently at a far more fantastic theory. According to his account radio waves originate in unimaginably powerful chain reactions perpetuating themselves at almost the speed of light and destroying entire galaxies just as a nuclear explosion destroys atoms. He believes that the high-intensity radiation of a supernova contaminates upon impact any heavenly body with which it comes into contact, transforming it into a supernova, and that this process repeats itself until a whole galaxy has been destroyed. A chain reaction of this kind would indeed be plausible in the relatively dense center of a galaxy. However, such a cataclysm is almost impossible for us to conceive of. The assumption of life upon an as-yet-uncounted number of inhabited planets would lead to the implication that millions and millions of cultures would be destroyed by such a catastrophe—a doomsday far more horrific than anything postulated by even the grimmest religions of our planet.

The Soviet physicist V. L. Ginzburg is of the opinion that radio waves originate not from disintegrating galaxies but from galaxies in the process of formation. A cloud of proto-matter contracts and causes the formation of several galaxies. Cosmic rays generated by this contraction strike the gas of the cloud, releasing high-speed electrons that generate the radio waves. Ginzburg's theories are based on exact calculations, and seem to provide at least a partial explanation of radio waves.

The probability is therefore that there is not just one but a number of explanations for the origin of radio waves. They always seem, however, to be generated by catastrophes of unimaginable vastness, thus proving that the universe has not yet reached a stable, stationary state.

THE INCOMPREHENSIBLE GALAXIES

The galaxies influence each other. Exact scientific investigation of this phenomenon has shown that the energies at work have nothing to do with gravity as we know it. Other kinds of energy must be involved that exercise their effect only over immense distances and upon very large masses. Up to now nothing is known about what these energies may be.

Observations have led to the further conclusion that under the influence of these unknown energies galaxies behave like viscous fluids. And yet a galaxy is constructed out of extremely thin matter that in theory cannot behave at all like a viscous fluid. No explanation for this phenomenon has yet been found.

Equally incomprehensible are the "stellar bridges" that connect the galaxies to one another. These young, oval, bluish white galaxies, discovered in most recent times by Soviet astronomers, present immense difficulties in the way of understanding. They emit an unusual radiation that is not in accordance with the laws normally applicable to spatial bodies emitting radiation.

In general it may be said that so far as their dimensions and masses are concerned the galaxies differ strongly from each other. Some have a diameter of 7000 parsec; others extend up to 40,000 parsec. The number of stars varies between 10^7 and 10^{12}. Spiral-shaped and elliptical galaxies are known, as are miniature galaxies circular in shape. A good middling distance between two galaxies is about 500,000 parsec. Probably no two galaxies are completely alike, just as no two stars or no two men are completely alike. It is difficult to understand how the same laws of nature could have led to such differences in results. The temptation is to suspect that in the universe the laws of nature are much less stable than is generally believed.

WHAT HAPPENS INSIDE THE STARS?

The individual stars are even more varied than the galaxies. In all probability there are invisible stars of superdense matter that are no bigger than the size of a human fist yet have the same mass as our sun. It is certain that there are stars a million times brighter than the sun (S Doradus, for example), and others that are only one-700,000th as bright as the sun (as for instance the dark companion of the star Wolf 1055). There are stars 2000 times larger than the sun and others as small as our moon.

On the other hand stars vary only a little in mass. The smallest are about one-twenty-fifth, the largest about fifty times, the mass of the sun. Surface temperatures range between 40,000 and 1000° C. (it is 6000° C. on our sun). In books of popular science the statement is often made that temperatures in the interior of stars often reach several million or even billion degrees. The fact is however that we do not know what goes on inside the stars; it may be that our concepts of temperature and matter are not even applicable. The general surmise is that the suns construct other elements out of hydrogen after causing the atoms to melt, thereby releasing and radiating energy of huge intensity.

These processes are under precise investigation. The research will inevitably raise numerous questions to which no answers have yet been found. For instance how can stars construct an element like technetium, which has an average life span of only 250,000 years, when the presence of this chemical element can be documented on stars which are already billions of years old? No known nuclear reaction could lead to such a result. Is some sort of "alchemistic" transmutation process in play? Do the elements, like stars, have their origins in explosions of proto-matter?

The universe conceals more secrets than has ever been imagined. Research into them has only just begun. How large is the part of the universe accessible to us? There are differing opinions even on this point. If the speed of light represents an upper limit on velocity, then man will not be able to travel further than ten light-years even with photon rockets. Jean Charon is of the opinion, however, that the speed of light is by no means the upper limit, that the entire universe is indeed accessible to us, and that in time man will be able to fly as far as the Andromeda nebula and back to earth again. If this theory is true, then posterity will be able to travel through extensive regions of the cosmos and assuredly experience many surprises.

—Jacques Bergier

Parapsychological Research in the Soviet Union

Other worlds apart from our own, which for topological reasons have no means of communication with ours except through telepathic phenomena, are now achieving some recognition among psychologists.

—Professor G. B. C. Stueckelberg

SURPRISES ARE DUE

Reports emanating from the Soviet Union in recent years indicate that hypnosis and telepathy are regarded as scientific facts. According to Soviet professor Vasiliev, director of experiments in telepathy carried out at several research institutes in the U.S.S.R., the brain of a hypnotist is a kind of radio transmitter, whereas the brains of his subjects function as receivers. His experiments prove fairly conclusively that the subjects obey the orders of the hypnotist even when he is in a different room, a different house, or even another city. Telepathy can be easily explained, according to the professor: if one brain sends strong signals to another, the receiving brain must be able to pick them up without difficulty.

The consternation of the French rationalists is the consequence of their complete ignorance about the status of Soviet research and the evolution of scientific thought in the Soviet Union. Since 1917 research work has been strongly intensified. In the meantime parapsychology has gained acceptance at the universities. The history of this development has been told by a Soviet author.

THE SILVER SPOON AND THE MATERIALIST

Bernard Bernardovitch Kaschinski is an electrotechnologist. For the past forty years he has been involved in all research work on telepathy in the Soviet Union. His principal opus, *Biological Radio Communication,* was published last year by the Ukrainian Academy of Sciences in Kiev.

51

Kaschinski's interest in parapsychological phenomena derives from an unusual experience.

In 1919, when he was living in Tiflis, his best friend fell ill of a fatal disease—the doctors diagnosed typhus. During a hot August night Kaschinski was suddenly awakened by what sounded like the noise of a silver spoon striking glass. He looked around in his room for what had caused the noise, but in vain. The next afternoon he learned that his friend had died during the night. He went to the dead man's house in order to see him for the last time. There he saw, on the night table next to the bed, a glass and a silver spoon. Seeing him look at these objects the dead friend's mother told him through her tears, "I was just about to give him his medicine. At the very moment when I put the spoon to his lips his eyes went blank. That is how he died. It was pre-ordained that he should not take his medicine again."

Immensely moved and excited, Kaschinski asked his friend's mother, amidst apologies, to demonstrate to him exactly what had taken place. She put the spoon into the glass, and when it touched bottom it gave off the same sound that Kaschinski had heard during the night at a distance of more than a mile. In what mysterious way had the tone communicated itself to him across this distance and in spite of his deep sleep?

Kaschinski is not a superstitious man; he is a confirmed materialist. But on that day he swore he would solve the mystery, and one day would know what had gone on in the mind of his friend's mother and in his own mind. Under the famous scientist Alexander Vassilievitch Leontivitch he began to study the human nervous system. He collected facts and came to the conclusion that the human nervous system is capable of reacting to stimuli whose source is as yet unknown, and in 1923 he published a book entitled *Thought Transference.* The book interested a number of scientists, but the two men who showed the greatest interest were not scientists.

DOES THE EYE EMIT RADIATION?

One of them was the Russian science-fiction author Alexander Belayev, the Soviet Jules Verne. Using the research of Kaschinski as his foundation, he wrote a novel, *Lords of the World,* which became a bestseller in the Soviet Union. Many young people were influenced by the book and began to interest themselves in telepathy. It can be said without exaggeration that *Lords of the World* had the same significance for telepathy as *Twenty Thousand Leagues Under the Sea* had for the submarine.

The second man interested in Kaschinski's work was Vladimir Leonidovitch Durov, one of the most famous animal tamers of his time. His experiences had convinced him that it was possible to communicate thoughts to animals. During 1923 and 1924 Durov conducted ten thousand experiments under the supervision of experts. He succeeded in communicating orders to animals, for instance, getting them to pick up some object and bring it to him.

These experiments were evaluated statistically. It was calculated that the probability of a success being attributable to chance stood at sixteen to ten million. The most skeptical animal psychologists were totally convinced. However, the intellectual climate in the Soviet Union at the time was not especially sympathetic toward experiments of this kind, and when the results were published, they made little impact. Work on them has continued only in the most recent times. Today the Soviet Union is looking for people who, like Durov, possess the unusual ability to communicate their thoughts to animals.

During the training sessions it was established that Durov's brain radiated high-frequency waves over the wavelength 1.8 millimeters. Unfortunately, at that time the instruments used to establish and measure such radio waves were still extremely primitive, and it was therefore not possible to document the existence of this radiation with any scientific exactitude. Durov may not have been a scientist, but he was certainly a sharp observer. Among other things he was convinced that the eyes of men and beasts radiate rays. He had noticed that the human gaze can tame the wildest of animals. In addition he ran experiments on the well-known but nevertheless still unexplained effect of staring at the back of a human being's neck: he chose people who had no idea what he was up to and fixed his gaze immovably on the backs of their necks. In 100 per cent of the cases the person so stared at turned his head.

Durov challenged scientists to track and prove the radiation emitted from the human eye, but proof was never successfully achieved. In the meantime, however, his work has been continued. The Soviets now believe they can document the existence of radiation emanating from the eye of one individual and absorbed by the pineal gland of another.

Such a theory calls to mind the legends of the "third eye," as the Soviets are well aware. Kaschinski cites a book published in 1907 in Russia by the Indian Ramacharaka in which the pineal gland is already called a telepathic "receiver." In 1959 a report was read at a physiologists' congress in Buenos Aires to the effect that electrical stimulation of the pineal gland on a human guinea pig had generated illusory light impressions. Durov had made precise investigations of the manifestations of paralysis evoked in certain reptiles and fish by the gaze of men. This research is being taken up again today in the Soviet Union, where it is hypothesized that the eye emits an electromagnetic ray. The wavelength of the beam is put at eight-hundredths of a millimeter, somewhere between radio waves and infrared rays. The beam is thought to be a powerful compression of rays, with a part of the eye acting as a directional force.

Since such waves project in a straight line and are blocked by non-translucent objects, they do not of course explain the phenomenon of telepathic communication over large distances. But if it can be proved that there is radiation released from the eye and received by the pineal gland, then even in the present stage of research many traditionally held attitudes in psychology will have to be abandoned. As Kaschinski rightly says, physiologists and brain specialists will be obliged to take long-distance causes and effects into consideration.

FIELDS OF ENERGY AND THOUGHT TRANSFERENCE

Soviet scientific research has been increasingly open-minded toward such phenomena since the beginning of this century. In the last thirty years several studies have been published on investigations into thought transference and rays emitted by humans. Of special significance is an article by Prof. S. J. Turlugin that appeared in Leningrad in 1942. Turlugin showed first of all that the effect of the human gaze is nullified when an ultra-fine-meshed piece of wire netting is placed between the "transmitter" and the "receiver" (nape of neck of second man standing within eyeshot). He then went on to show that the radiation can be reflected by means of very fine defracting nets, but not by metal mirrors. From these findings he drew the conclusion that the radiation emanating from the human eye must be made up of electromagnetic waves of extremely short duration, highest-frequency waves of millimeter length. The results of Turgulin's research were tested at the time by P. P. Lazareff, a member of the Soviet Academy of Sciences. The great physiologist Ivan Petrovitch Pavlov had established similar phenomena. Today research is being continued in various directions. The purpose of one investigation is to settle the question of whether mescaline or some other hallucinatory agent can serve to stimulate radiation from the eye.

The Pavlov Institute pursued research into telepathy and into the reactions of various organisms to waves of different kinds even in times when such activities were not looked upon with approval. In 1959 Petrov discovered that magnetic fields of high frequency affect the higher nervous system, alter reflex actions, and cause feelings of pain. Today such investigations are carried on quite openly. Dr. W. A. Kosak of the Pavlov Institute takes the position that phenomena such as thought transference and emotions generated across large distances are effected by fields of energy that are not necessarily electromagnetic in nature.

A PROGRAM FOR RESEARCH
INTO PARAPSYCHOLOGICAL FORCES

Research of this kind is by no means a monopoly of the Soviets, but a part of the investigation conducted throughout the world into the forces that form living substances. These forces oblige the atoms and molecules within and sometimes without a living organism to keep to well-defined tracks. This phenomenon seems to work against the laws of chance as we usually conceive of them. It has not yet been possible to develop an instrument that can be used to document the existence of this force, yet countless experiments have led to the conclusion that there must be such a force. For instance, Professor Weiss of New York University demonstrated in an experiment that a piece of down from a feather bed, disintegrated, reconstructs itself when soaked in a culture medium. The molecules out of which the down is put together are clearly ordered according to a set pattern by some field of energy. Secondary effects of this field of energy manifest themselves as phenomena that are electrical in nature.

Is this field of energy the same one in operation in thought transference? The possibility is not to be excluded. At any rate, we now know that an organism can react to stimuli that do not present themselves in the usual way.

The Pavlov Institute has conducted a series of highly astonishing experiments along these lines. A volunteer is positioned near an electrified stepladder. When he touches the ladder, he gets an electric shock accompanied by a high-frequency sound signal inaudible to the human ear. The experiment is repeated many times in this manner. The current is then switched off, but the sound signal repeated whenever the volunteer touches the ladder. Even though the ladder is no longer electrically charged, the volunteer jerks back his hand as fast as possible. The case is clearly one of a conditioned reflex. Yet how did the sound signal get into the volunteer's nervous system, since it was not audible to him? And even if it is assumed that somehow the signal penetrated his subconscious, it is still not clear why a repeated electrical shock was necessary to sensitize him for the signal. For Soviet scientists that is the kernel of the problem.

Once the scientist knows how the subconscious can receive signals that have not passed through the consciousness yet are demonstrably substantial in character (ultrasonic waves can be measured with crystal), then, according to the Russians, he will also understand telepathic phenomena, which in their opinion are merely an expansion of human faculties of perception into the unknown. Seen in this way, telepathy is not a manifestation of an immortal soul or of a ghost, but rather a material property of human existence, therefore subject to investigation with all the precise means of science. A Soviet research program is now being set up accordingly. Telepathy is only one of many phenomena investigated. The reaction of the human body to electromagnetic and ultrasonic waves is also a part of the research, along with the subject of hypnosis and the possibility of a return to the past under hypnosis.

In the context of this program Dr. L. B. Kompanejez succeeded in returning a sixty-three-year-old woman to her eighth year. Not only could this woman remember the most trivial incidents of a day that lay more than half a century back in her mind, not only did she write in an orthography no longer in use since the revolution, but she could also see perfectly without her spectacles for the entire duration of the experiment. Clearly hypnosis sensitizes certain areas of the brain and body, among them the as-yet-unidentified telepathic "receiving organs." These receivers are quite certainly material in nature and can therefore theoretically be localized. The Soviet scientists, at least, are firmly convinced of it.

MAGNETISM AND HYPNOSIS

Included in the research work now being carried out free of the former secrecy are the investigations of Professor Vassilyev, regarded today as the Nestor of parapsychological research in the Soviet Union. Vassilyev, who has been occupying himself with these problems since 1921, is a specialist in physical phenomena in the upper atmosphere and in electromagnetic fields; he is director of the Institute for Theoretical Physics at Leningrad University.

Vassilyev's first experiments were concerned with phenomena that he discovered in 1921 and that still have not been clarified. The problem arises from the following: Using a horseshoe magnet placed about 2 inches from the nape of the neck of a volunteer under hypnosis, it is possible to confuse optic images suggested to the volunteer that do not exist in reality. However, this effect can only be obtained if the north pole of the magnet is held behind the right temple, not if it is held behind the left temple—that is to say, it will not work when the poles are reversed. There is no way for the volunteer to know that a magnet is behind him, and the director of the experiment gives no explanation or description to the volunteer of what he is doing. The results are invariably the same. Lately an explanation was believed to have been obtained through the experiments of the French scientists Sadron, Douzou, and Polensky. The three researchers claim to have established that the nucleic acids, which play so important a part in hereditary processes and in the memory, possess magnetic properties. But the results of their experiments contain some inconsistencies, and so we have to confess that the phenomenon discovered by Vassilyev has not yet found a convincing explanation.

How can a magnetic field have an effect upon brain structures which correspond to a suggested image? Why does the image seem to move? We still do not know the solution to this puzzle. All the same it is possible to be sure that telepathy is merely a special case of a very widespread phenomenon. Through hypnosis or conditioned reflexes we can make the body sensitive to forces it does not usually perceive: magnetism, ultrasonic waves. The telepathic field of energy probably consists of a whole series of physical forces. Which part of the body, in man or animal, receives the magnetic forces, the ultrasonic waves, the telepathic messages? We do not know. However, is it not true that we are discovering new components in our cells and brain every day? In this regard the Soviets ascribe great importance to the researches of the German scientist Kirsch, a specialist in research on neurons, or nerve cells. Kirsch claims to have found in the neurons structures resembling a radio receiver with antenna and detector. His opinion, however, is widely disputed; a number of papers on the subject have appeared in the Soviet Union.

WIRELESS RADIO COMMUNICATIONS BETWEEN BRAINS?

Whenever there is talk of telepathy the obvious implication is communication effected through electromagnetic waves and especially through radio waves. Most American parapsychologists reject this viewpoint: they want to prove that telepathy is a manifestation of the immortal soul. This attitude, however, is not scientific but philosophical. The mystery can only be solved by sticking to the facts.

In many of the early experiments in telepathy conducted over large distances no provision was made for protective measures designed to block the transmission of waves. Experiments with various protective measures were carried out, but it is doubtful whether any of the measures was effective enough to stop high-frequency short waves. Today it is known, in contrast to earlier assumptions, that electromagnetic waves transmitted over the wavelengths between 1 millimeter and 1 meter are capable of extension beyond the horizon by means of multiple reflexion. It is true that this kind of extension happens only rarely, but then telepathic manifestations are rare too. Many Soviet researchers use this argument in support of the hypothesis that telepathy is dependent upon rays or waves emanating from man. Other Soviet scientists reject this hypothesis out of hand. Professor Arcadyev, who has calculated the amount of energy the brain is capable of radiating, believes that the amount of energy produced is so small that it would lose its impact after just a few meters. Arcadyev confirmed the results of research by the Americans W. K. Volkers and W. Candib, who discovered in March 1960 that muscular contraction gives off electromagnetic signals. But these signals are extremely weak. Highly sensitive instruments can pick them up if they have not traveled more than an inch or so. Even if the human brain (or the skin or the complete nervous system) were more sensitive than the finest measuring instrument—which has yet to be demonstrated—an electromagnetic thought transference from brain to brain over a distance of more than one meter is difficult to conceive of. For that reason many Soviet researchers find the hypothesis based on electromagnetic waves untenable.

They are probably right. If the human organism were a receiver for electromagnetic waves, then some sort of psychological or physiological effects upon the engineers and technologists working constantly within close range of high-frequency, high-voltage radiation plants would surely be noticeable. But nothing of the kind has been noticed. A few extraordinary manifestations observed in connection with radar installations can easily be explained. Most cases are of rising body heat, or climbing temperature, due to the absorption of electromagnetic waves. Other cases are of equally well-known chemical reactions that occur under exposure to high-intensity radiation. For the time being at any rate the hypothesis that there is an electromagnetic explanation for telepathy must be rejected.

STATUS OF RESEARCH IN THE SOVIET UNION TODAY

Research on telepathy in the Soviet Union is carried on primarily at Leningrad University, in the Institute for Physiology directed by

Professor P. I. Gulyayev. At the moment the scientists are not publishing regular bulletins on their research results.

The results obtained so far prove only that telepathy is possible when the volunteer acting as receiver is placed under hypnosis beforehand. The research program of the institute is divided into the following areas: the investigation of telepathic manifestations between twins; control of machines by telepathic signals; stimulation of the nervous system by radiation of various kinds; investigation of telepathic contact between two volunteers, both connected to an encephalograph; direct notation of thoughts.

Czechoslovakia has an Institute for Parapsychological Research, directed by D. Ryzl, and an institute has been founded in Poland; but it is in the Soviet Union more than anywhere else that parapsychological research receives the approval of a broad sector of the population. Once a series of research results is confirmed, the researchers can probably expect substantial state subsidies for the continuation of their work. These scientists are a step or two ahead of their colleagues in other countries insofar as they work from strictly scientific premises. They are not trying to prove that there is such a thing as a ghost. Nor are they trying to make political capital out of their work in the manner of American researcher J. B. Rhine, who has called parapsychological research a "weapon against Communism."

On the other hand their materialistic orientation leads them to deny the possibility of the existence of other parapsychological phenomena like soothsaying and telekinetics. Tactically speaking, perhaps that is a good thing: it is probably wiser, if they are not to offend the state agencies, to tackle one phenomenon after the other rather than all of them at once.

But telepathy alone threatens to burst the bounds of recognized science. If it does in fact function independently of distance, if it does not belong in our system of space and time, then a lot of rethinking will be necessary in psychology, physics, and chemistry.

If there is such a thing as "psychological space" that transcends our continuum of space and time, if "distances" can disappear within this new concept of space as soon as one brain is attuned to another, then we will be obliged to construct a new cosmogony. And it is beginning to look as though telepathy can only be explained on the basis of such a supercontinuum.

—Jacques Bergier

Are There Intelligent Beings Beyond the Earth?

It is indeed very possible that mankind is controlled by automated intelligences from another world.

—Roger MacGowan

Nobody demands that a literary critic be capable of writing a second *Remembrance of Things Past;* instead he is allowed to stand for what he is: an avid reader of books with taste and judgment, a layman with some expertise. It is a quite different story when a non-scientist dares to direct reasoned criticism at science: the majority of professional scientists immediately object.

On the table before us is Volume 255 (1962, third and fourth quarters) of the *Proceedings of the French Academy of Sciences.* In this publication famous specialists have specialized in trivialities. Nourishment for our dreams is as absent from its contents as it was from Volumes 254 and 256. And if our dreams are not being nourished, is the cause of science, at least, being advanced? That is more than questionable. Not one Nobel prize in the sciences has gone to France since 1935. Could it be that something is wrong with the spirit of our research? At any rate we "friends of the wondrous and chroniclers of wonders," to borrow Maurice Renard's phrase, believe that French scientific research is not likely to regain the reputation it once had with learned contributions like "The Influence of Incubatory Warmth on the Artificial Synthesis of Certain Steroids in the Testicles of Rats." No doubt this article represents a solid piece of work—but it is a little narrow in perspective in a time when man stands on the threshhold of the cosmic age.

FROM THE TINY TOPINAMBUR TO THE MIGHTY GALAXY

Before the next twenty years are up mankind will have made contact with intelligent beings from outer space. They will without doubt not be living organisms but rather some kind of thinking machines. There is a great deal of reason to believe that these intelligences already have us under observation. Everything points to the fact that they control us. That should be sufficient cause for us to be prepared.

The author of these lines is not even remotely a pupil of the quick-minded genius Charles Fort, collector of "cursed facts." He is neither a science-fiction writer nor an enlightened UFOlogist. We can assure you that he is just as serious a scholar as the rat researcher mentioned a moment ago. His name is Roger A. MacGowan, and he holds a responsible post in a manufacturing plant in Redstone, Alabama, where atomic warheads are produced to help maintain the equilibrium of fear. The essay that contains the statements cited above is called "On the Possible Existence of Otherworldly Intelligences." It contains numerous mathematical formulas, diagrams, and sixty-six references to the latest publications on this subject. It appeared on eighty pages of fine print in Volume IV of *Science and Technology of Space,* a publication for scientists put out by the New York University Press and edited by the leading Western specialists in the field. There is no publication with better credentials. We hope that we "Sunday scientists" may be forgiven for giving our attention more to such publications, which seem to exude a breath of the cosmos, than to the majority of French periodicals, which seem to have run out of breath, printing articles like "The Effect of X Rays on the Roots of Topinambur" or "Summer Anomalies in the Melting Point of Air."

INTELLIGENCES FROM OUTER SPACE

Efforts to pick up communications from otherworldly intelligences are completely legitimate. Once the large radio telescopes are in operation the efforts will undoubtedly be successful. That will happen in ten or at most twenty years.

MacGowan holds the opinion that on certain planets within our solar system there are non-human, automatized intelligences. The British astronomer Fred Hoyle has even gone so far as to postulate that the giant masses of dark cloud in outer space are a kind of consciousness. MacGowan does not take up this somewhat lyrical hypothesis, but starts from a theory by Holmberg, who in 1938 discovered sixty planets revolving around other suns outside our solar system. He arrived at the conclusion that 67 per cent, or some 130 billion of the stars in our solar system, are surrounded by planets. If that is true, then our galaxy is swarming with life.

LIFE OLDER THAN THE STARS

But how did this life start? Where did it come from? Several Soviet and American authors have recently begun to discuss once again the possibility of an artificial paninsemination of the earth. They believe that life on our planet developed from "fragments" of life left here by visitors from another world. The astronomer Thomas Gold from Cambridge put forward the thesis that life on earth originated from the leftovers of a picnic of intergalactic space travelers. MacGowan does not exclude the possibility that life was brought to earth from elsewhere, either intentionally or by accident. But in his opinion it is still important to go into the question of whether life perhaps did evolve independently on this planet, and he feels the appropriate experiments should be conducted. Why should life not have come into existence spontaneously? It is well known that Pasteur rejected this theory. But MacGowan believes that this rejection, based on religious convictions, held back scientific progress for a century.

Louis Kervan believes in the possibility of biological mutations. His hypothesis has not yet been proved, but if it should turn out to be correct, then life would be nothing more than a simple alternation of physical and chemical processes. The mutations would have been brought about by something else, by some other force, a belief held already by the alchemists of antiquity. Elements stable in their natural state lose their stability, according to Kervan, as soon as life enters into the game. This theory would bear out Pasteur again in his rejection of the possibility that life began spontaneously as a series of physical and chemical reactions; he would then stand aligned with tradition as well as in agreement with the latest research.

The possibility is there that life has existed for all eternity, and that it came to earth, like space and time, before everything else. "O life, older than the stars themselves," say the Holy Scriptures of India.

THE MOON, MARS, AND VENUS

What proof do we have that there is life outside our planet? Charles-Noël Martin is convinced that "there are an infinite number of worlds and forms of life in existence." MacGowan has occupied himself solely with our more immediate environment: the moon, Mars, and Venus.

According to a 1960 essay by Gilvarry, the dried-up oceans on the moon contain organic sediments. Tektites, mysterious glasslike masses that are to be found on earth, are from the moon and were hurled into space by lunar volcanic explosions.

Photographs communicated by space satellites have not yet been able to provide us with clearly defined information about the vegetation on Mars, but from all appearances, during spring on Mars the edge of the vegetation belt advances ten miles every day.

As for Venus, there are many theories in currency at the moment:

1. The planet is covered by a jungle of low-growth plants, similar to the vegetation on earth during the Mesozoic Era.
2. The surface of the planet Venus is a wind-whipped desert.
3. The planet is submerged in a substantial layer of petroleum, in which tiny organisms swim.
4. A sea formed of water containing heavy carbon dioxide envelops the planet like an ocean of Alka-Seltzer.

MacGowan makes frequent reference to Professor Nagy, who with his team of researchers proved that the meteor that fell into the community of Orgueil during the last century contained organic substances.

FROM THE BIOLOGICAL TO THE MECHANICAL EVOLUTION

Life in the neighborhood of our planet, if it exists at all, is clearly still at a very rudimentary stage of evolution. But on far-off planets, where life is billions of years older than on our planet, it must have reached an unimaginably high stage. Taking the known facts of today and the present state of evolution of mankind as his starting point, MacGowan made a projection of how astonishingly far intelligences of so much greater an age must have developed. Then he established a law intended to be valid for our world and for other worlds:

As soon as biological life becomes endowed with intelligence it begins to replace the biological components of its being with mechanical components. Then intelligent beings evolve, automatons which think exclusively mechanically: mechanical evolution has taken the place of biological evolution.

That is the shape of our future, according to this outstanding expert, a military man as well as a scientist. Elsewhere this future may already be present.

We cannot share this viewpoint, since it seems to us highly questionable whether artificial modes of thought can ever completely replace natural thought processes. At a certain stage in the evolution of technology it will certainly be conceivable, but can it take place without doing violence to thought itself? Could such artificial thought grow and perfect itself without the eternal life it probably will possess? Philosophy stands therewith at the great divide, today as it did yesterday, and today its dilemma is more acute than ever before.

For MacGowan, clearsighted man of machines and of streamlined schemes, perfection and renunciation of life are one and the same thing. Permit us to summarize once more his view of what evolution will look like:

Man is the starting point. Then comes the Cyborg, the robotlike creature, fitted out with electronic organs, that is half a living organism and half a machine. It may be that one day science, in its battle against death, will provide fully transistorized hearts and introduce into our circulatory system a mechanical aid that can never fail. The next step, according to MacGowan, will be from the Cyborg to the completely electromagnetic being, a robot programmed by the human brain. Finally the brain itself is displaced. The robot programs itself, develops itself, and provides the nourishment for its own intelligence. And so mind, divorced completely from the flesh, will have attained the goal of pure domination.

ON THE ESSENCE OF THOUGHT

In his study, remarkable for the breadth of its horizons and its scientific sobriety, MacGowan also analyzes the essence of thought and postulates a series of general equations in an effort to define its process. According to him the following factors can be isolated:

> deduction
> introspection
> induction
> memory
> sensations and instincts
> feelings

He demonstrates that the various organs of sense and thought perception can be replaced by mechanical and electronic devices, and that such ''organs,'' fed with the appropriate information, not only can think and feel but can also remember. However, the human brain contains 10^{10} neurons, which can digest and use information with a speed not yet attained by any electronic computer.

MacGowan believes that comparable electronic brains can be built in the foreseeable future. But is it true that the thought processes are limited to the factors listed by MacGowan? What about:

> extrasensory perception
> intuition
> attunement to wavelengths of the future
> memory older than ourselves
> analogous thinking
> . . . ?

What about the indefinable something that makes man more mysterious than his own spirit, that raises him above it, that makes him far more complex than all equations, and through which he wants to express his special place in creation?

Is thought only concerned with information? Is it not rather concerned with information plus the significance of that information? MacGowan, limiting himself to what can be observed and wanting to examine the mind under an absolutely cold light, says No. It is possible to go along with him only if human psychology in its entirety is taken as restricted to behavioral psychology. It is not possible to go along with him if the subconscious and unconscious layers of the mind are taken into consideration, and especially not if the supraconscious layers are taken account of.

RESERVES OF INFORMATION IN OUTER SPACE

Today electronic computers need a thousand million seconds to find something in the memory which the memory itself can find in one-tenth of a second. But MacGowan is not mistaken in believing in a quick rate of progress. In 1939 all the treasures of the earth would not have been enough to buy a gram of plutonium, yet in 1962 a gram could be bought for eight dollars. Progress has been made in leaps and bounds over the most varied areas of knowledge during the same period, achieving advances, if multiplicatory calculations were used as a measure, corresponding to ten million times the starting point. Machines that have digested information comparable to that contained in a brain and are able to ''communicate'' with each other by means of electromagnetic waves over wavelength frequencies of between 20,000 and 100 million hertz, would have the advantage over man, whose means of communication is language. Such machines, MacGowan thinks, would form a much more productive and more cooperative society than any grouping of biological beings. He is clearly of the opinion that such machine societies exist already on other planets and that man, should the speed of light not represent the ultimate velocity (Jean Charon's hypothesis), will make contact with such societies within the next thirty years.

His theory is that intelligent automatons have set up stations approximately five or ten light-years from the earth, in which huge reserves of knowledge are stored to be available for our use. But we do not yet know how to get at these reserves or how to send out the sort of signal that could release them. The opening up of these reserve depots should be one of our first priorities. He believes that every star that is neither frozen nor molten but inhabited by biological or mechanical life emits infrared rays over wavelengths between eight and twelve microns. The suggestion of this specialist for atomic warheads is that man should begin as soon as possible to build huge telescopes constructed to pick up these infrared communications. In his opinion this endeavor would make a lot more sense than radio astronomy, a science of recent date, which restricts itself to radio waves from the cosmos.

RECEIVERS FOR EXTRAORDINARY TRANSMISSIONS

Have we had visitors from such space stations? MacGowan repeats the well-known claims, cites old legends, and considers it to be quite possible—though he offers no new proofs—that such visits have taken place. It may be that intelligent automatons have left no traces of their visit. Are they waiting until the inhabitants of the earth are more interested in them? Are they waiting until the earth has transcended the primary stage of biological life?

MacGowan thinks it probable that automated devices journey through the solar system to observe the planets, collect information, and feed it back to their home planets. He cites several articles by the Australian professor Bracewell in which mention is made of fragments of radio or television programs being receivable days, weeks, or even months after their original transmission, without its being possible to establish the origin of the electromagnetic waves. Possibly something somewhere in outer space picked up the programs and redirected them to another world for information purposes. One of Professor Bracewell's scholarly papers has the astonishing title "On Receiving Communications from Higher Galactic Societies."

The temptation is to postulate a different hypothesis: Time is perhaps not of so simple a nature as man has believed; its texture can perhaps be modified, enabling words or pictures of a transmission from radio or television to be heard or seen years later. One is reminded of the two Englishmen who suddenly and without warning saw before them the park of Versailles as it had been in the eighteenth century. But this hypothesis, being non-materialistic, has not been formulated either by MacGowan or by Bracewell.

FROM MacGOWAN'S MACHINES TO CLARKE'S BUTTERFLY

Installations at present in service for receiving signals from outer space have a maximum range of 8.7 light-years. Radio telescopes, when perfected, will be capable of sounding out the approximately 2000 stars within a radius of less than 100 light-years. MacGowan believes that every intelligent being, biological or mechanical, tends to transmit waves on the 21cm wavelength; the intergalactic hydrogen gas clouds transmit on this wavelength. Bracewell too is convinced that a network of communications exists along this wavelength in our galaxy, linking the automated space stations with those planets inhabited by biological or mechanical intelligences. According to MacGowan the otherworldly intelligences are only waiting for us to discover this interstellar communications network; then they will establish communications with us.

These societies are observing us, know what stage of evolution we are at. Is there any reason why they should not destroy us? For them we are hardly born. Arthur C. Clarke has some beautiful words on this subject:

Since only the structure is important, cannot mind and intelligence exist and function without the hindrance of matter? Can they not, like electronic currents and radiations, exist in a relationship between pure quintessentialities of being? In this way the mind, which has been formed through interactions with matter and has used matter as its transporting element for so long, could one day climb out of this matter as the butterfly climbs out of its cocoon. And just as the butterfly soars up towards the summer sky, so the mind could take flight in experiments of a scope not in any way comparable with that of its former transformations.

Clarke's vision of the future is imbued with an almost religious fervor. MacGowan's picture on the other hand is icy cold; he ends his postulations with four tactical conclusions:

1. Either our biological society of mankind will be transformed stage by stage into a society of robots;

2. or mankind will quickly be controlled by the robots it builds;

3. or mankind, if it delays much longer, will be destroyed by intelligent otherworldly robots;

4. or mankind will be helped, supervised, and controlled by mechanized, otherworldly intelligences.

OUR SOULS WHISPER IN THE SHADOWS

Reading MacGowan's essay arouses to a certain extent feelings of horror, yet it must be recognized as an outstanding piece of work, accomplished by a specialist entrusted with a position of great responsibility and not afraid to investigate the "true fictions" of our time. We do not however share his sense of resignation and hopelessness. We believe that man should tolerate no other master except himself. We believe that man sees behind machines the shadow of the capabilities he must himself attain. Future evolution, which without doubt will include the wonderful, still unresearched human "machine," is already casting its shadow over the world of engineering. "These are images of the future God, not God himself."

—Louis Pauwels and Jacques Bergier

The History of Electronic Brains

No machine can lie,
But so can no machine speak the truth
—G. K. Chesterton

PRESENT AND FUTURE STATUS OF THOUGHT MACHINES

A few years ago in the fall the slopes of the Himalayas were swarming with people. Thousands and thousands of Chinese were at work, carrying baskets full of stones and gravel, building roads intended to open the way up to the roof of the world, no longer Tibetan territory. Perhaps this Chinese struggle belongs in the realm of the spirit, but that is not the issue here. What is important is that this battle of a thousand-year-old culture against the modern world has set mankind back five thousand years.

In the field of thought, however, we in the West are still at the stage of the Chinese with their baskets; most of our scientists and scholars carry their entire "raw material" around with them in their heads. They still work without the aid of machines. But we are experiencing the final hours of this manner of living and working.

Man has invented tools that extend his capabilities: in the bathysphere he can dive into the depths of the ocean; in the spaceship he can explore outer space. Electronic computers permit him to attempt tasks for which his mind alone would not be sufficient.

We must be clear from the very beginning about what is to be meant by "thinking machines"—the term often generally used for these tools. If man is a wonderful and still partly incomprehensible machine, then we share the opinion of Louis Pauwels that this machine will never be surpassed—except by himself. We do not and cannot believe that there will ever be machines capable of displacing and replacing man. We believe that on the contrary man will invent more and more new machines that will serve mankind. We believe that man, in the

73

course of his psychic evolution, will never abdicate his power in favor of steel monsters. That is the kernel of the philosophical problem; everything else is idle rhetoric. We are convinced that artificial thinking will never take the place of natural thought processes. One fact is certain: the human brain is not composed merely of matter and energy. Time is also one of its components. It is the result of an evolution of life over three billion years. A brain constructed by us artificially, whether from metal or crystal, will have one decisive deficiency: it will lack the time factor accumulated in the course of the process of evolution. We are too young. In other, infinitely older worlds, living beings have perhaps indeed been replaced by machines.

But let us return to the here and now. Already machines exist that can digest thought processes in large doses and establish connections between the digested items of information in an astonishingly short time. Such machines open up new possibilities to the human mind. Above and beyond the machines known today, which are veritably miraculous to our present way of thinking yet merely fragments in comparison with what future developments will bring, it is possible to envisage instruments that elongate and strengthen the human mind as a crane strengthens the arm. A real revolution has begun in this area of human knowledge, albeit of recent date. Let us draw up an interim balance sheet.

THE MAN WHO LIKED QUIET

The history of machines constructed to help and support the human mind began in 1642 with the calculating machine invented by Blaise Pascal, which was capable of doing additions. Thirty years later Leibnitz built a machine capable not only of adding but also of multiplying. He used a numerical system based solely on the digits 0 and 1 (it was constructed around the powers of 2); it is designated as the binary or dual-digit system.

In this system the sequence of digits of the traditional decimal system is used in the following way:

1	2	3	4	5	6	7	8	9	10	11	12	13
1	10	11	100	101	110	111	1000	1001	1010	1011	1100	1101

The numbers in the dual-digit system are composed of approximately three times as many digits as those in the decimal system; for that reason this system is not particularly well suited to the human brain as a system for working with figures. But it is perfectly suited for a mechanical brain. Such a machine has only two alternatives: it can answer "Yes" or "No," using the symbols $+$ or $-$, 1 or 0. When the current is switched on, it gives the first answer; when there is no current, the second. The big and complex computers combine a large number of electronic switching devices.

In the nineteenth century operating calculating machines built according to the Leibnitz model appeared on the market. They were constructed and perfected by inventors like Thomas of Colmar, Léon Bollée, Monroe, and Friden.

Also in the nineteenth century an eccentric Englishman named Babbage devoted his life to two aims: building a gigantic calculating machine and fighting wandering minstrels. He felt that the out-of-tune singing of these street musicians was a disturbance to the work of the mind and was having a paralyzing effect on culture. They allowed him enough leisure, however, to invent a calculating machine based on the principles of Jacquard's spinning wheel. It was constructed like modern machines, with an artificial memory (the information vault), a reckoning mechanism, and a control system. All that was missing in Babbage's contraption was electronic tubes. But they had not yet been invented.

Half a century later, in 1880, Hollerith invented the punch card.

Around the same time a second eccentric genius emerged, the American Strowger.

. . . AND THE MAN WHO HATED THE TELEPHONE OPERATOR

Strowger was the proprietor of an undertaking concern in Chicago. Just as Babbage had despised wandering minstrels, so Strowger bore a relentless hatred for telephone operators, those girls in the telephone exchanges who set up the connection between the calling parties. He commissioned one of his nephews to devise a machine that would make the exchange girls superfluous. The nephew invented the telephone dial, which connected the line of the caller automatically with the line of the party he was calling. For the first time a true calculating machine could now be built. The punch cards were its memory, the electronic tubes its automatic dialing system, and the lines went to the nerve cells of the automatic brain. Before 1937, however, there was no epoch-making advance; the only memorable contributions were the researches of two Frenchmen, Valtat and Couffignal, on the dual-digit system.

The first modern electronic brain was put together in 1937 in a small college in Philadelphia, the Moore School. The inventors, two American scientists named Eckert and Mauchly, named the machine "electronic numerical integrator and automatic computer," ENIAC for short. The computer contained 30,000 tubes, an immense number in those days. The significance of ENIAC was twofold: firstly, electronics was used for the first time in the construction of calculating machines (opening up the possibility of completing calculations at the speed of light), and secondly, a system for digesting information or figures was built in—designated as the "memory" of the computer. The designation is unfortunate because it calls to mind the human memory, with which it has in reality nothing to do. ENIAC was intended for the American armed forces; it was supposed to serve in range-finding calculations. But the calculations were not completed until nine months after the end of the Second World War, and by that time the army had lost interest.

ONE OF THE GREAT GENIUSES OF OUR TIME

In every branch of knowledge there are periods during which progress is made at an accelerated pace. New ideas crackle the air, researches undertaken independently of each other begin to project similar aims and results, discoveries and inventions abound. The decade 1937–1947 was such a time. On June 28, 1946, the Institute for Advanced Study in Princeton, New Jersey, published a work over the names of John von Neumann, Arthur W. Burkes, and Hermann H. Goldstine. It was a decisive work for the future of electronic brains. In it the technique of programming was described. The problem was not only to feed numbers into the machine, not only to accumulate a memory bank, but to program the machine to use the data with "understanding" in a manner appropriate to solving the question posed. Their technique even permits the machine to include in its calculations a figure that it has not digested, but that it may possibly need in the course of its operations. A program is not necessarily a sequence of linear operations joined together like the links on a chain. It has to allow for divergences, for new information that can modify the import of other information.

Alongside the mechanical advances so necessary for the construction of modern machines, methods of programming were developed during this decisive decade. The English and the Americans discovered the magnetic-drum storage plant. Dr. Alexander of the National Bureau of Standards developed storage elements in which elastic waves can be used as signals that reproduce themselves in quicksilver. At the University of Manchester the use of cathode-ray tubes led to the development of so-called electrostatic storage cells. At last punch cards and punch strips became obsolete in computers, and were replaced by real electronic memory banks.

During the same period studies were carried on on the concepts of logic that these modern machines make possible. We owe most of these concepts to one of the extraordinary men of our time, the mathematician John von Neumann. This Hungarian-born man was until his death in 1960 the "brain" of the United States on matters concerning domestic economy and defense. The extent of the esteem in which he was held may be gauged from the fact that during his last illness (he suffered from an unusual form of cancer contracted probably as a consequence of the effects of radioactive radiation he was exposed to on an inspection visit to nuclear reactors) his bedside visitors included the most prominent politicians in the land, from the President to ministers and high officials. Although he was suffering indescribable pain, he continued to the last, thanks to a superhuman strength of will, to pass on counsel about top-secret research projects and the development of an economic and industrial system in which there would be no more economic crises.

John von Neumann postulated general concepts simultaneously embracing physics and psychology. He started by investigating the theory of games like poker, chess, and bridge. Certain possible practical applications of his works, through which the concept of strategy is generalized, gave him the chance to work out the theory of electronic computers.

AS SIGNIFICANT AS E = mc²

Thinking machines were conceived originally solely as calculators. Calculating is without doubt extremely important. Man builds bridges, nuclear submarines, spaceships, airplanes, and automobiles; to build them, he needs calculations. The first machines constructed to help him perform these calculations are still in service. They are an important aid to research and technology.

Since 1947, however, it has been known that electronic computers can deal with not only numbers but with information of all kinds.

The term "information" is a general concept, defined in the modern sense by Leo Szilard, Claude Charon, and Léon Brilloin. The digit is only one of many forms of information; other forms are the dance of the bees, language, music, art, coded messages. Once it had been understood that any piece of information can be defined mathematically, it was recognized that electronic computers are capable of many things hitherto undreamed of: translating from one language into another, looking up a certain word in a book, deciphering a message of which the code is not known.

Information is neither matter nor energy. It can be defined mathematically with astonishing ease when the importance of this concept is borne in mind. The mass of information is equal to the result of the following equation:

$$\frac{\text{Probability of an event or state after receiving the information}}{\text{Probability of an event or state before receiving the information}}$$

For the future of mankind this equation is as significant as Einstein's $E = mc^2$.

With its help a competent mathematician can demonstrate why crossword puzzles are possible, can interpret the dance of bees in honeycombs, can work out a frequency ratio permitting communication with the planets Mars or Venus, can build an electronic computer capable of absorbing information of all kinds, not just numbers, which can play chess, dance, study, translate, analyze. It is true that such a machine cannot think (a point which cannot be made often enough), but it is so many-sided and adaptable that it can be of real help to man, and open up new possibilities for the human brain.

FASTER AND FASTER THINKING

After 1947 the territory of electronic computers was flooded: more and more new machines poured out. They performed their tasks with an ever-increasing speed. Bendix has already announced a computer capable of absorbing 100 million items of information per second. He intends to use in its construction the latest electronic invention, the Dioden tunnel (similar to the transistor, but in practice not subject to fatigue). For such a machine the only limit is the speed of light; it is capable of absorbing information faster than the human brain. It would be capable of following what happens in the interior of a nuclear explosion even before the explosion actually takes place. At the present time there are no electronic computers of this type on the market, but the data-processing installations available today, for instance the Gamma 60, already accomplish astounding things. One of these installations in the Comptoir National d'Escompte in Paris services 30,000 bills of exchange every day in four hours, work that formerly took 100 people a full day to accomplish. Account supervision is in the process of being totally computerized. More than one million accounts will then be under automatic supervision, with only one installation needed, the Gamma 60. In two hours it can complete a task for which punch-card machines needed 200 hours.

MAGIC CUPBOARDS OF TODAY

We have witnessed a number of these computer installations in service: in Paris, Brussels, Milan. It does not seem appropriate to call them "machines." At first glance a Gamma 60 looks like a large, bare, antiseptic room resembling an operating room. In the center two men sit at a desk. They communicate with the machine by means of a keyboard similar to the keyboard of an electric typewriter. The keyboard can be activated either by Gamma 60 or by the operator whenever he wishes to feed in another piece of information. The installation itself consists of a row of steel cupboards arranged around the room without any obvious order or any visible connection. As many cupboards of this kind can be put together as are felt to be required. Only one cupboard is absolutely necessary, the central unit containing the control mechanism. In contrast to the human brain, this control mechanism can concern itself with several problems at one and the same time. It has an unlimited number of parallel "subconsciousnesses." The effect is the same as if a scientist were able to think simultaneously of problems in physics, chemistry, mathematics, and biology. The center cupboard contains a memory bank of ferrite nuclei and a series of electronic switch elements to control the cupboards connected to it and make possible the simultaneous accomplishment of several tasks. A ferrite nucleus is tiny; its diameter is not even one millimeter. Ferrite is a chemical fusion of iron oxide and other metal oxides; it is able to store information through magnetism.

Its storage capabilities adapt themselves to what is needed. A storage bank of this type can accommodate up to 200,000 digits, which can be released at a speed of 6 digits per one-hundred-thousandth of a second.

The working elements have the following tasks:

1. They process information; the arithmetical element conducts calculations using the figures supplied by the storage bank.

2. They store information; the magnetic tape store can take up to 10 million pieces of data (digits or letters), and up to 24 machines can be connected up.

3. They feed information into the installation (storage unit) and give information out (retrieval unit); several punch-card, ticker-tape, or modern telex machines can be connected to a single installation.

The cupboards arranged about the room around the center unit make calculations, combinations, work things out, then deliver their results. To communicate with them, the operators go through the center unit. This machine has a language of its own consisting of mathematical symbols for its own internal use, and a series of simpler languages to use for communications with the outside world.

1200 MILES OF LITERATURE PER HOUR

With such a computer installation it is possible to run a bank or an insurance company, collect all the words in a given language in a dynamic store for study or translation, calculate flight patterns for interplanetary satellite explorations, and make it possible for the human brain to achieve new syntheses in the most varied areas.

The electronic processing of information provides an opportunity to make the impossible become possible. Research projects or industrial reorganizations that once seemed too complex now become capable of accomplishment. In our time we are witnessing serious men engaged with problems that five years ago were still the province of science fiction: bankers are interested in electronic data-processing installations; linguistics experts are studying the dual-digit system; military men want to have the track of a rocket traveling at colossal speed calculated in less than a second, or an exploding nuclear device analyzed. The necessary provisions have not yet all been made; the processes of communicating with the computer, *i.e.* the input and output of information, are still a great deal slower than the operation of the computer itself. However, rapid printing systems have been developed that can print up to 1200 miles of paper per hour with symbols understandable to the programmer. For the future the prospects are even more fantastic.

MACHINES WITH CHARACTER

On a March day in 1959 the American scientist Dr. A. I. Samuel lost a game of bridge. It was a memorable day in the history of mankind. For Dr. Samuel's opponent was an IBM 704 computer. This electronic computer had been programmed in a new way. A "study program" had been fed into it. After ten hours the machine played a better game of bridge than the author of the program.

Research projects on this subject are being carried on with special emphasis in the United States, for instance, in the Corbell Aeronautics Laboratory in Buffalo. It is extremely difficult to work out programs of this kind; for every single one a whole team of specialists is required.

At Euratom a team of researchers is at work on the development of an electronic computer that can play chess. The work is being undertaken not because of the game but because such a computer could also control one of the nuclear reactors that are planned for construction over the next twenty years in nuclear energy plants.

Machines capable of learning also possess an undeniable "personality," and some major firms have hired psychologists who are specialists in the psychology of three-year-olds. Does that mean that such an installation is capable of thinking? No, assuredly not, but it does demonstrate certain "behavior" tendencies. Remember that even swords and sailing ships had "character," and were given names and treated like living creatures by their owners. Racing cars too, even though far less complicated than data-processing installations, have "personality," and some only perform at their best when a certain driver is at the wheel. From the time of the very first tool a kind of symbiosis has always existed between the tool and its user. And the more perfect the tool has become, the more complex and intimate this relationship.

MACHINES WITH A SHORT TEMPER

Like small children, electronic computers sometimes turn out to be wicked and whimsical. Occasionally their "fits" can be explained scientifically. One computer would only work with the window open. After months of examination the designer discovered that he had paid too little attention to the cooling system. With the window closed the room became so warm that the transistors did not function properly any more.

The lesson was learned: Gamma 60 is now fitted with 6 cooling units that keep the temperature of the element constant at 14° C.

Another computer registers interference whenever castanets are played in its neighborhood, which means it is highly sensitive to movement. An installation in the United States rejected the program fed into it with the comment: "That is absurd; you have tried to divide 0 by 0."

Data-processing installations do not always protest in so spectacular a manner. But even the tiniest error is enough to throw the entire program out of kilter. A French expert, Jean Porte, writes:

The first attempt at programming always results in a depressing show. Either red lights start going on all over the place while the entire installation stalls, or else it doesn't stall but instead the program runs its course for ever and ever through the same cycle of false data. Or it delivers incomprehensible printouts.

A single mistake is enough to render a complete program worthless; and when a machine is getting old, errors easily occur. For that reason the "inoculation" of machines against mistakes is being seriously considered. The method of doing this will be to feed in a number of possible errors along with a study program designed to indoctrinate the machine against ever repeating those errors.

TOMORROW THEY WILL SPEAK OUR LANGUAGE

Data-processing machines, unlike the human brain, can if necessary be rejuvenated. It is enough to replace the deficient parts. In principle they can also learn from their mistakes. In this direction a number of research projects are in progress under headings difficult to elucidate: modernization program, interpretation program, occasional cells, majority logic installations, threshold-communications functioning. It is impossible to provide a simple account of these highly complex projects. Suffice it therefore to say here that they are concerned also with a kind of "inoculation" that would have the purpose of ensuring that an error once committed could not be repeated. The machine keeps check on itself according to the principle that three like results over three different circuits must be accurate. An electronic computer incapable of error is already on the horizon.

Soon men will no longer communicate with data-processing machines through electronic keyboards but through language. The installations will have devices to translate the language of men into the language of machines and vice versa. American scientists, notably Anthony Oettinger, have already made significant progress in this direction. "Brainstorm sessions" between man and machine will be taking place in the near future. Anyone familiar with the data-processing installations of today is, however, bound to look forward to the plants of the future with some misgivings, and the necessity of psychotherapeutic treatment for such computers is an idea which perhaps does not belong entirely in the realm of fantasy.

AGAINST TIME AND SPACE

Today there is a great deal of interest in the possibility of direct communication between man and computer. Studies on the subject take various viewpoints. On the one hand a new language is sought that would allow for a better direct contact between man and machine. Mathematicians like the Dutchman Hans Freudenthal have developed "Lincos," which is intended also to facilitate communication with other minds, with for instance the inhabitants of other planets.

On the other hand an effort is being made to improve the feed-in machines. The punch card, the keyboard, even the human language, need too much time. If the installation could be supplied with data with the speed of television pictures, that is to say as fast as pictures appear on the screen, it could then receive information in one minute equal to the contents of a whole book. For projects such as the one planned by the University of Nancy, namely the feed-in of all important works in the French language (together with vocabulary, grammar, and the most significant literary masterpieces) into one single data-processing machine, such speed would be a timely boon.

Other technologists and scientists are concerning themselves more with the output mechanisms. The human word is here again too slow. The installations must be in a position to communicate with each other in a language of their own. One approach to this problem is through the installations of the telephone networks. Even today approximately 40 per cent of new telephone connections are being set up not between men, but between data-processing machines.

Future data-processing installations will be able to establish their working units thousands of miles from the center element. Already installations are being planned which have the center element on the earth and working units on the moon, on Mars, and on Venus. In this way technology will have succeeded at least in part in conquering time and space.

DIALOGUE BETWEEN MAN AND MACHINE

I put a question of enormous interest to me to a dozen technologists, all specialists in the theory of information and data processing at the Bull Corporation.

I asked them, "Do you believe that one day there will exist a world memory, a giant brain that will control and rule mankind in the manner sometimes described in science fiction?"

The technologists seemed very doubtful. They do not believe there will ever be one single information center with such power; the work they are doing is intended to develop less costly, smaller installations. Modern man no longer makes the journey from Paris to Marseille on foot; he uses transportation. Future man will not think on his own; he will use a portable data-processing machine that will evaluate information for him. Such machines will be of enormous value especially for scientists and technologists. They will be "personalized": each individual will possess a machine attuned exactly to him, which knows him absolutely precisely and supplements him as far as is possible. The machine will also be informed about his failings and weaknesses, will know, for instance, that he is in the habit of omitting exact proofs because he is unable to cope with certain mathematical formulae, and will therefore provide him with the formulae and their resolution. The infinite patience of the machine will give to the work of the scientist an exactitude, finality, and comprehensiveness unattainable without its aid.

From this perspective the machine will be of great help to man. But on the other hand man will have to work hard to make possible a cooperation that is fruitful and without friction. Close collaboration between man and electronic computer will enable man to work out general ideas, set up categorical concepts, and develop his capacity for abstract thinking to an extent hitherto undreamed of.

The men who collaborate with machines today are called programmers. Among them are a few highly gifted specialists, but the present training for the job is not likely to awaken the creative imagination necessary if the cooperation between man and machine is to be fruitful.

THINKING MIRRORS

Technologists today are especially concerned with the storage units of data-processing installations. At the present time storage is mainly on magnetic tape. The data so stored can be recalled in a few split seconds. But however extraordinary these units are, they no longer satisfy the specialist. Attempts are under way to develop mirrors in which billions of items of information—called "bits" by the experts—can be stored. Some of the experimental storage units being built in the laboratories seem straight out of a fairy tale. Among them is the "remembering mirror," developed by K. Kallmann and J. Rennert for the United States Marines. It consists of a specially composed crystal surface that absorbs everything it "sees," even in complete darkness, since it registers the infrared rays that all objects and living creatures radiate through their own warmth. It is a genuine magic mirror out of fantastic literature, that black mirror that Cocteau said "had to think carefully before it reflected the image." Truly, this mirror thinks.

Electrons are used in other storage units: their track within the atoms permits the notation of data. This is perhaps the basis of the ability of chromosome molecules to bear hereditary traits. In other experimental storage units the hyperconductivity of matter at temperatures near absolute zero is used. Some storage units are veritable libraries: the automatic library at IBM contains one million printed pages per unit, and such units can be put together in unlimited numbers. In every unit the desired document can be called in one second, and the photocopy is ready in five to ten seconds. Building an electronic memory bank that would hold all the information accumulated by a man in the course of his life—a mechanical version of Proust's "time remembered"—is not a technological but a financial problem.

All these memory banks are static; they do not themselves change, nor do they ever change anything they have stored away, in contrast to the human mind, which somehow, in its most mysterious innermost recesses, shades everything it stores. But work is being done, at least in theory, on dynamic memory banks in which the stored data would change, and the stored bits of information interact among themselves.

CONNECTION TO A NETWORK OF KNOWLEDGE

The concept of the personalized data-processing machine—along with the possibility of setting up such individual units of a major installation thousands of miles apart from each other yet to connect them with each other—is the first step toward establishing connection to a network of knowledge, a connection that one day will be a fact of life as much taken for granted as today's connection to the power plant or the water supply. Every firm, every laboratory, and many households will have such a connection, which will make it possible to put questions by telephone or telex that will be answered by a data-processing installation far away. A network of knowledge of this kind will help the solution of economic, industrial, and commercial problems as well as other matters.

Today a laboratory without power and water connection, without compressor and evacuator, is unthinkable. Very soon it will not be possible to imagine a laboratory unconnected to the network of knowledge.

Charges for using the network can be computed by means of automatic devices similar to the meters used nowadays to calculate electricity and telephone bills. The day of the ivory-tower research scientist will be over forever. Every researcher will be able to share the findings of every other researcher and be able to confirm the accuracy of his ideas and projects. From a certain stage upward in the hierarchy of intellectual life every individual will possess, in addition to his connection with the network of knowledge, a special miniature machine attuned to him personally, as an aid to his thinking.

We believe that evolution will tend in this direction, toward automatic machines that aid man's thinking, extending and accelerating it. It is not probable that mankind will go in for an artificial "superbrain."

As a counterbalance to the imaginative but bleak vision of the future postulated by MacGowan we would like to present a more human, dynamic vision put forward recently by an electronics expert in a professional journal:

Today already electronic rays are weaving the net of a common will to learn between man and the universe, between the universe bursting with possibilities and man filled with the desire to learn.

—Jacques Bergier

The Four States
of Matter

*The horizon opened up to matter.
Darkness created clarity.*
—Maurice Leblanc, *Les Trois Yeux*

DO WE KNOW THE STRUCTURE OF THE UNIVERSE?

The first man to surmise that there was a further state of matter apart from solids and liquids was Johann Baptist van Helmont (1577–1644). Van Helmont was on intimate terms with miracles. The stone of wisdom had been donated to him anonymously, and with its help he manufactured several hundred grams of gold. In 1609 he refused a university professorship in order to remain free to devote himself to what he called the "philosophy of fire." In honor of alchemy he christened his son Mercury. This son edited his works and recorded his experiments. Van Helmont demonstrated the existence of gases, and showed that matter can be reduced to a state thinner than fluidity, that it can become an invisible "steam." Gas is invisible but strong. He exploded iron containers by compressing gas in them with a pump of his own invention. After thirty-five years of experiments he was able to prove conclusively that there exists a third state of matter apart from the solid and the liquid, namely the gaseous.

If there are three states, then why not four? Many scientists have concerned themselves with this question, in particular William Crookes toward the end of the nineteenth century. Crookes's colleagues cast a wary eye on his sanity because he interested himself in levitation, telepathy, and spiritualism. And yet his surmise was correct: there is a fourth state of matter, in which it is still more gaseous than in gas. This fourth state is designated as plasma. (It has nothing in common with the blood fluid of the same name.)

In a normal gas matter is present in the form of stable molecules or atoms. In plasma the atoms have lost some of their electrons; in technical language, the matter has been ionized. Plasma is therefore composed of the usual molecules and atoms, along with ionized molecules and atoms and some free electrons. Where is the borderline between gas and plasma? There is no clear borderline. The physicist talks of plasma whenever a considerable number of atoms have lost their electrons (in physics a "considerable number" would be 10^{10} to 10^{20} ions per cubic centimeter).

A SCIENTIFIC WORLD OF ITS OWN

There are many visible examples of plasma around us. It blazes out from advertising lights and from the tubes of neon lighting. It streams down upon us from the surface of the sun with unbearable brightness. Plasma is generated and exists normally under quite well-defined circumstances: strong electrical discharges, exposure of atoms to strong radiation, very high temperatures. It is visible in very bright flames. These need not be any hotter than other flames, but must simply contain a substance that is lightly ionized. Anyone can create plasma completely safely by strewing ordinary cooking salt through the flame of a candle. The heat of the flame is not great enough to separate the electrons from the sodium molecules. The flame is composed of the usual combustive gases, ordinary sodium molecules, ionized molecules, and free electrons. And so we have a plasma before us. This new composition possesses unusual properties, of which traditional physics and chemistry had no notion. The theory of plasma is extremely complex. To understand it knowledge of advanced mathematics is essential. Not all properties of the fourth state are known; scientists all over the world are actively engaged in researching them.

A few simple examples will serve to show that the scientist who concerns himself with plasma enters a completely new world. Whereas ordinary gases expand and try to fill any given space, plasma can be made to contract under certain conditions by means of electrical (balled "lightning") or magnetic forces. From earliest times there have been reports of fireballs caused by thunderstorms that crashed through houses and gave off electrical shocks on exploding. As late as 1935 the possibility of such a phenomenon had been neither confirmed nor denied by scientists. But once balled lightning had been successfully generated in the laboratory, it had to be recognized as a reality. The latest theory of plasma proves that the eye-witness accounts going back to the most ancient times are in accord with the facts of nature.

Electrical charges in motion generate an electrical current. A current creates a magnetic field. In its turn a magnetic field influences the track of electrically charged particles. For that reason plasma can contract itself to form a vapor that repels other plasma vapors. These vapors are called plasmoids. The assumption has been made that the solar systems were composed of gigantic plasma vapors before they were condensed to suns and planets. It has been possible to generate plasmoids in the laboratory that bear a strong similarity to galaxies and that can even look like spiral vapors.

A GAS THAT BEHAVES LIKE A METAL

Ordinary gases conduct electricity very badly, as is proven by the fact that if the outer ends of plugs with a voltage of 110 or 220 are left uncovered there is no danger of a short-circuit between them. Plasma is different. A good electrical conductor, it behaves at one and the same time like gas and like a metal. Placed between two electrodes, plasma will conduct the current like a metal. That is what happens in neon lighting tubes and fluorescent lamps. However, a fresh phenomenon manifests itself at very high temperatures: a metal conductor overladen with current will melt; but plasma cannot melt, since it is already a gaseous substance. The powerful magnetic field of the current causes it instead to contract: the plasma vapor is transformed into a slender, glowing tube. This process is designated the "pinch effect."

It should now be clear that this fourth state of matter, known to scientists for only about thirty years, represents as it were the "primeval" state. About 90 per cent of all matter in the cosmos is plasma. Solid, liquid, and gaseous substances are therefore exceptions.

The sun, fire, the northern lights, and the interplanetary gases are all plasma. Almost all interstellar matter is plasma, as are the belts of radiation that encircle the earth. Neon light tubes contain glowing plasma. Radio waves of natural origin are generated by electrical changes in the plasma.

Plasma always shows the same properties and obeys the same natural laws whether it is very hot (several million degrees in the interior of the sun), very cold (in the upper atmosphere), very dense, or strongly thinned out.

WHY IS RADIO POSSIBLE?

The discovery of plasma has far-reaching implications. Physics and chemistry, basing themselves on the three states of matter traditionally known, become sciences of limited import and interest. Now that plasma is known, many scientific mistakes of the past can be explained. Hertz, for example, had demonstrated that the waves he discovered could never transmit a message. He believed that they could never travel a distance such as that from Paris to New York because, like light waves, they traveled in straight lines. When the Italian Marconi, who knew nothing of the scientific theories of the German physicist, succeeded in transmitting a message over a great distance using the Hertz waves, scientists were unable to explain his feat. The solution to the mystery was discovered only much later: the earth is encircled in the atmosphere by a plasma belt that reflects radio waves and bounces them back to earth. This statement is valid at any rate for waves of lengths between several miles and several meters, that is to say for long waves, medium waves, and short waves. Ultrashort waves, decimeter, centimeter, and millimeter waves pass through plasma. On these wavelengths communications can be established between the earth and the space satellites in the vicinity of Mars and Venus. Through these space satellites it is now known that there is not just one radiation belt encircling the earth, but several stacked up one above the other, as for instance the Van Allen belts at 1600 to 3500 and 8000 to 12,000 miles altitude.

The physics and chemistry of plasma are no longer local but universal sciences. Even in their present early stages they are of special significance for space exploration. Psychologists have established the strange fact that decisive discoveries and inventions seem always to be made at the very moment when mankind is in urgent need of them. Man discovered plasma at the time when he was preparing his launch into outer space, an adventure that could only be carried through with perfect knowledge of natural laws.

Above the atmosphere there exist further layers of plasma encircling the earth. On May 15, 1958, Sputnik III discovered the existence of a cloud of plasma encircling the earth, denser over the poles than over the equator and capable of descending to within 160 miles of the earth's surface. Later it was established that this plasma belt is beneath a second layer. The first layer starts at an altitude of approximately 160 miles and extends to almost 650 miles; its highest concentration lies over the equator. The second layer begins at 25,000 miles altitude, and it encircles almost the entire earth including the poles.

The second layer represents the greater threat to astronauts attempting to advance through the cosmos. But the lower layer is of immediate interest to us on earth because of its effects upon the communications network. It originates in the relentless bombardment of the atmosphere by particles from outer space and through the absorption of solar energy. In the upper atmosphere gases are not so dense, but there are still approximately 10 million particles to the cubic centimeter. When the particles are ionized through radiation or collisions with corpuscles, they lock into certain tracks in the earth's magnetic field. Like miniature satellites the electrons travel from east to west and the positive ions from west to east. In orbit they circle back upon themselves while moving forward, as do satellites. To an observer on earth this track looks like a spiral. The earth is therefore encircled by spirals of such origin, which embrace the lines of force of the earth's magnetic field. Many of these electrons attain temperatures of 10 million degrees. The ions are not so hot, but their energy is still powerful enough to split the molecules of the atmosphere and create northern lights.

This ionized layer is not visible to the naked eye. But it does exercise an influence on radio waves. Along the 20cm wavelength the effect is almost nil. But beyond the 21cm wavelength, which represents a window in the radiation belt, its influence becomes extremely intense. The long, medium, and short waves between 3000 meters and 24 centimeters are strongly affected. The effects are very diverse. Some of the waves are completely absorbed, others split, and occasionally the layer acts as a kind of mirror of the spheres, creating images. This is the reason the sputniks were accompanied by the ''ghost pictures'' that remained alongside them and radiated the same rays.

THE MOST EXTRAORDINARY DISCOVERY OF MODERN PHYSICS

It has been established by the use of ordinary radio telescopes that the sun is encircled by plasma and is itself composed of plasma. From time to time this plasma explodes and showers the earth with cosmic rays, magnetic fields, electrons, and electrically charged particles. These particles fill our entire solar system and cause a phenomenon that has been known to man only for a relatively short time, namely the solar winds. Satellites sent from the earth to Venus have mapped these solar winds.

Only a few years ago the existence of these solar winds was neither known nor even suspected. A student of Bruno Rossi said recently in Florence that his teacher regarded the solar winds as the most extraordinary discovery of modern physics. It is now surmised that they have a modifying effect upon the rotation of the earth. The further assumption is made that the atmospheric changes which cause tornados occur under their influence. They influence in addition the currents beneath the earth's crust, setting earthquakes in motion. These hypotheses are, however, not yet proven. Man is at present not in a position to draw up a map of the heavens incorporating these solar winds. Once again all he really achieves is the knowledge of how little he knows. The interstellar vacuum never existed except in the imaginations of nineteenth-century scholars. The universe is not empty but shot through with currents and forces about which we know practically nothing; the solar winds are only one of many phenomena in outer space.

Solar eruptions not only hurl these strange winds at us but also transform the elements. This process has been very carefully investigated. Observations by, in particular, Goldberg, Mohler, and Müller have established that solar eruptions of special magnitude can generate hydrogen. This unites with the cores of other atoms to produce heavy, new atomic nuclei. The sun, especially its surface and its atmosphere, can therefore be designated as a huge plasma factory in which various chemical elements are manufactured in large quantities. It would be of great importance for us to know just how the transformations take place, even though we will never be in a position to reproduce them on earth.

In the beginning, therefore, was plasma. It saturated the entire universe, and its condensation created the heavenly bodies, which grouped themselves into galaxies. Astrophysicists are gradually beginning to understand why the galaxies have spiraling arms. With the aid of radio astronomy it has been established that just as there are solar winds, so there are galactic winds. Streams of plasma push out from the center of the galaxy at a speed of 35 miles per second. The Australian radio astronomer Frank Kerr succeeded in discovering these currents in the vicinity of our sun; their speed there was 5 miles per second. The mass of gas created by such movement is of a volume great enough to form a new sun every year. The new stars in the spiral arms of our galaxy probably have their origin in such processes.

The American scientist Halton C. Arp, who works on Mount Palomar, has demonstrated mathematically that the plasma streaming outward from the center of the galaxy is held together by a magnetic field in the form of a tube and directed toward the spiraling arms.

NO SUCH THING AS AN INTERSTELLAR VACUUM: THE UNIVERSE IS SATURATED WITH PLASMA

Like the solar winds, the galactic winds sweep along magnetic fields enclosed in the plasma. These magnetic fields influence in turn the formation of the galaxies and their connection with one another. There is no more an intergalactic vacuum than there is an interplanetary vacuum. On the contrary, space is saturated with plasma, magnetism, gravity, and perhaps with many other forces of which we as yet have no knowledge whatsoever.

It has been possible through experimentation to observe some of these forces on earth. W. Bostick conducted experiments with plasma in a vacuum chamber and was able to observe the plasma forming itself into substances that he called plasmoids. Plasmoids are plasma vapors that take on the shape of spiraling mist and can have a length of up to 50cm; they are usually about 10cm in diameter. They radiate light, and can be photographed. The pictures obtained are enormously impressive. They permit man to see a miniature universe in a test tube. As the alchemists of old told us, "What is above is the same as what is below."

Once science begins to attain comprehension, it begins to want to take control. The fourth state of matter is to be found not only in interstellar space but also on earth. It is already in use in industry, and this development will be continued quickly. The possibilities for its application range from circuit breakers for high-voltage electrical currents to firing mechanisms for rockets, the direct conversion of heat into electrical energy, the production of thermonuclear energy, and the construction of high-fidelity loudspeakers, to give just a few examples.

Two Hungarian scientists, K. Simonyi and M. Uszoky, want to make artificial suns out of plasma. A sun so created would have a diameter of 1250 meters, an interior temperature of 100 million degrees, and a pressure of 1000 atmospheres. Each sun would radiate 3 x 10^{16} watts. They would be set up as artificial satellites at an altitude of 12,500 miles with their velocity so calculated as to give them the appearance of remaining stationary above one and the same point on the earth's surface. The positioning of such a plasmoid above Siberia or the Antarctic would create in these areas a tropical climate, making possible the resettlement there of several hundred million people. Is that just a Utopian idea? Setting limits to the possibilities of science would be presumptuous. Plasma may well change our planet more radically than aviation or the discovery of nuclear energy.

AN ALL-CONSUMING FIRE

Artificial suns of this type would be glowing fireballs. Plasma can vary in temperature from one extreme to the other. Intergalactic plasma for instance is very cold, while other masses of plasma reach temperatures of millions or billions of degrees. Matter of this degree of heat cannot be kept in a container of any substance known to us. This problem is reminiscent of the problem of the alchemists' acid which dissolved everything. How can we store a fire that consumes everything with which it comes into touch?

Experiments have been conducted to seal the plasma in "magnetic bottles." This term is the designation scientists have given to an invisible container of which the walls are formed by the lines of force of a magnetic field. Since this "bottle" is not composed of matter, it cannot be consumed by heat. However, in practice it is extremely difficult to generate a magnetic field dense enough to prevent the leakage of matter in its fourth state.

The name of the French scientist Siegfried Klein often arises when there are discussions of research in this field. My friend Siegfried Klein will surely not be angry if I compare him with Thomas Alva Edison, the great inventor of the past century. Like Edison's, Klein's results cannot always be elucidated scientifically. Yet even when they are astounding in character they are still easy to attain. One of the most astonishing of his inventions already in use in industry is "talking plasma." This instrument is distributed in France under the name ionophone and in the United States under the designation Ionovac. Plasma streaming out through the air vibrates under the influence of a magnetic field and generates tones without needing any metallic elements. It is the one and only instrument that makes possible the reproduction of notes at their natural, true pitch. The theory of it has not yet received any satisfactory complete elucidation—or at least none such is known to me. Several physicists, in fact, have demonstrated that such an instrument cannot be made, yet it is already in use and on the market. The ionophone is proof that plasma can be put to use and that with its aid things can be achieved that are still held to be impossible by the theorists. We will have cause in the course of this essay to give several reminders of this discrepancy between theory and practice.

In contrast to the ionophone, the miniature converter is not yet on the market. Once this instrument can be mass-produced, it will be possible to create power plants without steam vats, turbines, and generators. At the present state of technology it is necessary to bring a liquid—water or quicksilver for instance—to its boiling point in order to transform heat energy into electrical energy. The steam sets the turbines in motion, the turbines drive the generators, and the generators produce the electricity. This process is the same in the most modern nuclear submarine as in the ordinary power plant heated by coal.

This roundabout method is especially tortuous when nuclear energy is involved. An energy of high pedigree is then used—misused might be a more appropriate term—to generate banal heat. Would it not be possible to convert nuclear energy or heat directly into electricity? What comes to mind immediately when thinking of this question is the thermo-electrical effect (the Seebeck effect). If you take two pieces of wire each of a different metal, one platinum and the other copper, for instance, solder them together at two different points, heating one of the joints and either leaving the other at room temperature or cooling it, an electrical current will flow from the warmer to the colder point. Heat is thus transformed directly into electricity. For a century the Seebeck effect has been in use for measuring temperatures. Naturally its use in industry for the generation of power has been considered. But metals conduct not only electricity but also—in this case unfortunately—heat; electrical and thermal conductivity stand in a direct relationship with one another. For that reason the capabilities and productivity of such thermo-electrical units are limited. To attain high voltages a large number of wires have to be put together, which makes for a complex bundle of wires awkward to handle. If alloys are used instead of metals, the results are better; but on the other hand even the most efficient thermo-electrical element of this type, set up in Toulon, delivers only a little above 6 watts per square yard (the joints in this construction are heated by the sun). To build a power plant of this type heated by nuclear energy, thermo-elements would be required with a weight of several thousand tons, and even then the results would not be outstanding. Siegfried Klein, like the Americans Lewis and Reiss, hit upon the idea of replacing one of the two wires in the thermo-element with plasma. Such a machine is at this time being built in the laboratories of the French Nuclear Energy Commission. With its help it will be possible to convert the heat of a flame directly into electricity. If the experiment is successful and the performance of the installation satisfactory, the converter can be used to create fuel from any substance whatsoever, including turf and seasonal substances like straw. The Klein effect can be obtained with any flame by scattering into it salt close to evaporation point, thereby increasing the number of ions. Potash is often used for this experiment. The ionized gases given off by nuclear reactors also display the Klein effect, and it may one day be possible to convert nuclear energy directly into electrical energy.

If the Klein effect could indeed be successfully employed in simple, high-performance installations, then the invention of this physicist would reveal itself as equal in importance to the steam engine or the electric motor.

POWER PLANTS WITHOUT TURBINES

The Klein effect was discovered during the course of experiments. Other researchers start from theories and develop out of them plans for installations to convert heat into electricity. They use for instance the magneto-hydrodynamic effect. Magneto-hydrodynamics, pioneered by the Swedish scientist H. Alfven, belongs to the dozen new sciences that have arisen out of the systematic investigation of plasma. Alfven seems to have been the first to notice that in a neutral, electrically charged liquid like plasma the magnetic phenomena must necessarily have a greater significance than in an ordinary fluid liquid like water. The theory of magneto-hydrodynamics led to the early realization that with the help of an electrically charged flame moving at sufficient speed, a machine can be constructed corresponding to the dynamo, in other words an installation in which a conductor mobile in a magnetic field generates an electrical current. Immediately magneto-hydrodynamic research was taken up in the United States, the Soviet Union, and France. I have already seen a few of these generators. They are still relatively heavy; it is still too early to think of their driving an automobile or an airplane. The possibility should however not be excluded that they will displace traditional power plants in the near future. It is simpler to generate electricity by introducing electrodes into a test tube containing a mobile flame than to bring water to the boil, drive a turbine with the steam thereby created, and have the generator brought into play by the turbine.

PLASMA ROCKETS TO THE PLANETS

The magneto-hydrodynamic generator is still not at the stage of mass production. There are still problems concerning the fireproof capacities of the substance, its stability, and its thermal equilibrium. But these will be solved, and it is virtually certain that a quarter of a century from now the power plants of today which burn coal or oil, will be replaced by magneto-hydrodynamic plants in which heat will be converted into electricity without steam vats, turbines, and generators.

But now let us suppose we have a magneto-hydrodynamic generator running the other way around, using heat produced chemically or atomically to give high velocity to a beam of plasma. If plasma is fired out of a rocket jet, the rocket will then be driven by the recoil. That would be an electrical rocket. The first man to postulate a hypothesis along these lines was the German Moeckel in 1959. At present the propulsion force of such plasma rockets is still very small, but it will soon be powerful enough for certain interplanetary flights, for instance between the earth and Mars or Venus. What is important about this force is that it remains constant over a long period. A plasma rocket would first have to be transported beyond the pull of the earth's field of gravity and set into a track corresponding approximately to its desired flight plan. At that stage, not before, it could be fired. The thrust developed would be only one-thousandth of its weight on the earth's surface, but through its capability for constant acceleration it would reach a speed of 50 miles per second in 100 days' time. And by then it would be in the neighborhood of Mars.

If plasma could one day be harnessed for peaceful uses all the energy problems of mankind would be solved. Sea water contains enough heavy hydrogen to cover our needs for thousands of years. But the only possible way to harness it is by creating a plasma that contains the maximum possible number of heavy hydrogen atoms, heat this plasma up to 10 to 100 million degrees, then seal it into a "bottle" formed of electromagnetic lines of force to prevent leakage. Nobody has as yet succeeded in doing this. Or at least, experiments have not as yet yielded usable results. But the experts know that the prospects in this respect are good; this fact was demonstrated to them in a dramatic way.

In April 1956 the celebrated Soviet nuclear scientist I. W. Kurtchatov accompanied the then heads of the Soviet government, Bulganin and Khrushchev, to Great Britain. He was permitted to visit the Atomic Research Center in Harwell, where he held a conference at which he made remarks that were nothing short of bombshells. He let it be known that Soviet scientists had succeeded in attaining temperatures of over one million degrees without using nuclear energy. He revealed to his foreign colleagues, who were dumbstruck by what they were hearing, that a team of Soviet scientists from the Soviet Academy of Science, under the direction of L. A. Artimovitch, M. A. Leontovitch, A. D. Sacharov, and I. E. Tamm, had been able to generate unimaginably high temperatures by conducting an electrical current of more than two million amperes through a gas. When heavy hydrogen was used for the gas it was discovered that neutrons and X-rays were released by the current. The conclusion cannot of course be drawn that in this way a thermonuclear chain reaction was set off; if it had been, the container would have exploded immediately. But at all events a first step had been taken. The Soviet scientist announced that research was continuing and that there existed some hope that the problem would be solved.

A number of years have passed since Kurtchatov's report. During this interval scientists and interested laymen have witnessed constant ups and downs. The early announcement that the harnessing of plasma was imminent had to be modified later when it was realized that plasma was not yet under control and that it was consuming more energy than it generated. The Pinch discharge, which first the Soviets and then the English (at their ZETA plant) succeeded in generating, is not stable. The plasma lashes at the "wall surrounds" of the "bottle" like a fire-breathing snake, and destroys them. At the very best the plasma can be kept inside for only one-thousandth of a second. For that reason other installations have been developed. The "stallarator," for instance, is a magnetic field into which plasma is sealed. The field is generated not by a discharge in the plasma itself but by current-saturated conductors outside the plasma. Some results were successfully obtained using this setup. Inexplicably, however, the plasma disappears in the stallarator, without anyone being able to explain how it is converted into ordinary matter. The problem of a peaceful use of fusion energy is not yet solved. But I still believe that the prophecy of my friend Charles-Noël Martin, who says that thermonuclear energy extracted from plasma is a thing of the far-off future, is all too pessimistic; in my opinion we shall be in a position to make use of it tomorrow or even today.

The discovery of the fourth state of matter has not only lifted the veil on the secret of matter in the universe, but also is leading to the creation of new sciences and branches of science ultimately more practically significant than the present sciences of chemistry and physics, which were based on the three aggregate states hitherto known. A revolution in the sciences, as well as a revolution in technology, is around the corner. More exact knowledge about the structure of the world, its origin and its evolution, will be attainable. In consequence, our industry and our daily life will gradually change.

Recently it was conjectured that there exists a super-heavy plasma with up to 6×10^{38} particles per cubic centimeter. Such plasma could well be present in the interiors of proton stars, the explosion of which causes the formation of galaxies in pairs of matter and anti-matter. Between intergalactic plasma, in which there is only one single particle per cubic centimeter, and this super-heavy plasma, there is an unending scale of density masses in plasma. Science has explored at most one-hundred-thousandth of this new world. Thousands of years will go by before it has been completely explored. But the breakthrough has been made, and it took place in our time.

—Jacques Bergier

Genetic Research at Present and in the Future

How stupendous is this drop of sperm from which we are created, which contains within itself all the imprints, not only of the physical appearance but also of the thoughts and passions of our forefathers. Where does such a tiny drop accommodate so endless a number of forms?

—Montaigne

FROM MAN TO SUPERMAN

The Nobel prizes of 1962 clearly identified an epoch in the recent history of mankind. Two of the prizes, the Nobel Prize for Chemistry awarded to the Englishmen Max Perutz and John Kendrew, and the Nobel Prize for Medicine awarded to two more Englishmen, Francis Crick and Maurice Wilkins, and to the American J. D. Watson, demonstrate the significance attained by a new science—molecular biology. This science is perhaps the most important of all, since it could one day enable us to have children just as we want them, with their qualities of body, mind, and spirit established in advance, their talents for music or mathematics arranged for, as well as their temperaments and humor, heated or cool, athletic or quiet and contemplative.

Molecular biology opens up to man the prospect of one day being able to have children who are better, cleverer, and more capable than we are, and of successfully creating, by controlled mutation, a superior mankind—supermen in the best of senses.

It must not be forgotten, however, that this new science also proffers terrible possibilities, of which the thalidomide tragedy conveys only the barest idea. A future Hitler could form future generations according to his will and thereby perpetuate his tyranny eternally. No science has ever before conferred so dangerous a power. For the first time it will be possible to influence, change, and shape from within and in advance the body and mind of our progeny.

1936 can be designated as the year when molecular biology was born. The Austrian student Max Perutz came that year to Great Britain to undertake research. His father allowed him 500 pounds sterling per year on which to live. But the annexation of Austria to the German Reich and the occupation of Austria by German troops cut Perutz off from his source of income. Later, however, he was able to secure a fellowship from the Rockefeller Foundation in the amount of 275 pounds sterling. Meanwhile he had set himself an ambitious project. With the aid of X-ray techniques he planned to research the structure of the giant molecules in living substance. His finances were of course extremely tight for so massive an undertaking; and so it took several years before he had saved enough money to acquire the necessary equipment for the evaluation of the X-rays. It was 1947 before Dr. Perutz and Dr. John Kendrew, with whom he was later to share the Nobel prize, had built up a kind of laboratory of their own. It was in a barn on a dusty farm in Cambridge. They moved out of this laboratory only recently. With the sort of equipment ascribed to penniless scholars in science fiction they succeeded in discovering the structure of myoglobin, a complex protein to be found in the muscles. In the end myoglobin was shown to be a kind of knot in space. Subsequently they researched the structure of hemoglobin, that important substance in our blood that conducts oxygen to the cells and the tissues: hemoglobin turns out to be a sort of fourfold knot. Thus they came to the spatial structure of the large molecules in living substance. After this initial research Dr. Perutz decided on a bold project: to investigate the structure of the giant molecules that function as the carriers of hereditary traits.

A THOUSAND-VOLUME ENCYCLOPEDIA
IN ONE SPERM HEAD

Genetics, the science of heredity, was hardly thirty years old when Dr. Perutz and his assistant decided to go to work on the adventurous task of unveiling its greatest secret. Previous calculations had already shown that a thousand-volume encyclopedia would be needed to contain all the information necessary for the description of a newborn child—and yet this information is already all contained in the tip of a single sperm. It was already known that at conception, when the spermatozoon penetrates the egg and the separation of cells begins, tiny fibers appear in the heart of the cell: chromosomes, so called because they accept pigmentation easily. They are so minuscule that several million of them bundled together are the size of a grain of sand. In the human cell there are forty-six chromosomes. It has been known for a quarter of a century that chromosomes are the carriers of heredity. More precisely, the carriers are the still smaller genes contained in the chromosomes.

It has been possible to establish that chromosomes consist in the main of a chemical synthesis, deoxyribonucleic acid (DNA). This acid conducts the information that causes the cells of the impregnated egg to organize themselves to a living entity and form an organism.

In what form is this information stored? Dr. Maurice Wilkins of King's College, London, decided to analyze the DNA molecule with the aid of X-rays, following the method made public by Perutz and Kendrew. Using a simple procedure he created DNA filaments from a solution, in the same manner that artificial silk or nylon are manufactured. He then took some excellent X-ray pictures that resemble abstract paintings of light and shade. By means of brilliant hypotheses and patient calculations he succeeded in establishing the structure of DNA.

THE SPIRAL STAIRCASE OF LIFE

Wilkins discussed his theory with two Cambridge scientists, Francis Crick and James D. Watson. After long discussions they became convinced that the DNA molecule is shaped not like a knot, but in a spiral, like a spiral staircase, with a banister of sugar (deoxyribose) and a little phosphate and steps of two organic bases, of which one contains a single benzyl ring, the other two benzyl rings. The two bases, which together always form one step, are joined solidly to the banister but only weakly to one another, so that they can easily be separated.

When a cell divides, a separation takes place on the steps of this spiral staircase of life. The banisters drift apart and take from surrounding matter the substances needed for the construction of a

new, complete stairway. There we have the wonderful, simple secret
of life, discovered at last. When the hypothesis put forward by
Wilkins, Crick, and Watson became known, the great American
nuclear physicist George Gamow calculated how many possibilities
there are when every step on the spiral staircase is built of two different
bases, taking all known bases into consideration. That was in 1955.
His calculations delivered the result that the qualities of a person, from
the most obvious to the most hidden, could be accommodated on a
spiral staircase made up of several hundred thousand steps. The
correctness of his hypothesis was confirmed by experiment. The DNA
molecule of a very simply constructed virus, the T-4 virus, contains
approximately 200,000 pairs of organic bases.

At this stage biologists began to sense that the steps of the spiral
staircase represent a kind of code and that each organic combination of
bases could bring about the generation of a certain protein. Thus the
code in the spiral staircase of life determines the scent of a rose or the
color of a newborn baby's hair.

Further researches established that life only uses four bases:
adenine, guanine, cytosine, and thymine. Between the two banisters of
the magic spiral information piles up from the four bases of the genetic
code, leading to the formation of a virus or a man, a flying dinosaur or
a sparrow.

This is not the place to discuss the origin of the first genetic code two
or three billions of years ago. Was it simply the result of chance? Or
the work of God? Science cannot give the answer to the question why,
only How. Genetic information, however, exists. We shall see that it is
so well sealed off and so well protected against deciphering errors that
it takes extremely powerful poisons (like thalidomide) or very heavy
interferences (from radioactive radiation, for instance) to cause
miscarried evolution and the birth of a monster.

INFLUENCING LIVING MATTER

We are still not in a position to program genetic information into the
spiral of life, but we can take sets of information from certain cells and
transplant them to other cells. The most extraordinary experiment of
this kind was carried out in the United States.

Cells of human origin introduced into culture mediums were transformed by two American researchers. They modified one genetic property of these cells by bringing them together with ribonucleic acids taken from other human cells introduced into culture mediums.

Science thereby succeeded for the first time in altering hereditary matter. Up to then such experiments had been dared only with bacteria and certain metazoa. Bacteria extracted from DNA were joined with "receiver bacteria," which in this way received new genetic properties passed on in turn to their descendants. Mutations of this kind are particularly interesting because of the fact that the transformed bacteria are able to grow in an environment in which previously they would have been unable to live.

The American scientists discovered with their experiment a mechanism that is capable, along with reproduction, of modifying the genetic hereditary mass of a mammal cell, even of a human cell. The two men described the course of their experiment in exact detail in their report to the National Science Foundation.

How was the DNA able to adapt itself to the most interior cells of the "receiver bacteria"? The Americans say nothing on this question; probably they were not yet in a position to elucidate it. But such experiments already come close to being miracles. What will happen when one day we are in a position to manipulate the genetic code at will?

THE SECRET LANGUAGE OF LIFE: FOUR LETTERS AND TWENTY WORDS

Let us return to the deciphering of the genetic code. In what form does the problem present itself to us? To give our explanation more plasticity, we would like to draw a comparison. Let us assume that all living beings are like books; they are as different from each other as for instance the Bible is different from a commercial novel. The analogy is of course valid only if we always keep in mind that identical books do exist, but no two living beings are ever exactly alike.

Books are written with words. In the secret language of life there is an equivalent for words, a molecule called amino acid. Extraordinary, and also confusing, is the fact that the language of life knows only twenty words. All proteins are composed of only twenty amino acids. By what mysterious law were precisely these twenty chosen from among all the possible amino acids? We do not know.

An average protein contains two hundred amino acids, which correspond to the twenty used by life. All possible combinations of these twenty words, which determine every aspect of a living being from bacteria to man, are etched into the steps of the spiral staircase composed of other bases (adenine, guanine, cytosine, and thymine). The four bases of the steps we will designate with their first letters: A, G, C, and T. The signal transmitted to the cell with the order to build up this or that amino acid and subsequently this or that protein is always a combination of three of these four letters; it is transmitted from three steps on the spiral of life. The carrier of this complex signal is a single gene, which therefore must contain digited information of at least two hundred words (a single molecule is composed on the average of approximately this number). The gene count in the buildup of a virus can range from ten to several hundred. Bacteria have an average gene count of approximately one thousand. A human cell starts at around one million genes. All human cells, whether muscle or nerve cells, are sealed off in the elongated DNA molecules inside the forty-six chromosomes.

If the DNA of a single human cell could be stretched out to a thread, it would be almost fifteen inches long. This thread contains exact information, frequently repeated, for the composition of every one of us. It is formed at the moment the spermatozoon penetrates the ovum, and reproduces itself a few billion times before the organism reaches adulthood.

If three out of the four letters A, G, C, and T are combined in all possible permutations, a simple calculation will show that there are sixty-four possible different combinations, where already twenty were enough to form the twenty amino acids of life. From nature's point of iew the difference between twenty and sixty-four is a kind of safety margin allowing the instructions to be repeated as often as necessary until they are carried out without error.

Deciphering the genetic code depends on knowing the signals corresponding to the various amino acids. Here is a complete list of these acids: alanine, arginine, asparagine, aspartic acid, cysteine, glutamic acid, glutamine, glycine, histidine, isoleucine, leucine, lysine, methionine, phenylanine, proline, serine, threonine, tryptophan, tyrosine, valine.

To be able to decipher the genetic code completely we would have to know, for instance, whether CCG corresponds to analine or CGC to arginine. It should also be mentioned that combinations are being discussed and considered on the assumption that they are indeed so put together.

THE SPARSENESS OF OUR KNOWLEDGE

Two years ago it looked as though deciphering the genetic code lay beyond the capabilities of the human mind. No direct translation has been achieved as yet; even with the help of the electronic microscope or X-rays it is not possible to read what is inscribed on the steps of the spiral staircase of life. The problem has to be approached obliquely, through investigations of what is going on in the cell. A certain RNA (see p. 111) can then be introduced to see whether the protein which results corresponds to calculations.

Apart from Watson, Wilkins, and Crick, who showed the way, so many scholars have devoted themselves to research in this area that it is impossible to list them all by name. Outstanding is Marshall W. Nirenbert, director of the Department of Biochemical Genetics at the Herz Research Institute in the United States. Nirenbert succeeded in stimulating microbes to produce proteins for which there was exact knowledge not only of what amino acids went into their composition but also of that composition itself, that is to say, the way in which acids are arranged in the chain forming the protein molecule.

Working on the basis of his own researches and also the investigations of François Jacobs and Jacques Monod of the Pasteur Institute in Paris, he succeeded through deduction in deciphering the code—only partially, but extremely plausibly.

These researches have established, up to now, the following: corresponding to every amino acid generated from the cell there exists, on the steps of the spiral staircase of life, a signal consisting of three initial letters (which is to say, three of the four bases in the overall pattern). The signals are transmitted one after the other, and not combined into a quadrant or patchwork or a structural pattern from the language of human life.

There are however on the steps of the spiral staircase some signs that do not correspond to any of the amino acids that can be put together. Crick's opinion is that these signals are meaningless. Nirenbert thinks they mark the beginning or the end of an item of information.

Elements of the signals can be altered by feeding poison to the viruses or bacteria, acridine for instance. It is possible that the mechanism at work in this process is the same that led in the case of thalidomide to deformities in newborn children; this surmise, however, is not confirmed.

By means of such changes a team of Crick's colleagues, Leslie Barnett, Sydney Brenner, Richard J. Watts-Tobin, and Robert Shulman, succeeded in carrying out experiments on the T-4 virus attacking the germ *Escherica coli.* The bacterium is consumed in twenty minutes, and about one hundred viruses exactly like the original virus have been generated. Every one of these viruses consists of a single "spiral staircase of life" with around 200,000 steps and a protective cocoon formed of six different sorts of protein. Each of the protein substances contains the twenty fundamental amino acids of which we are all composed. The structure of the T-4 virus can be easily changed through mutation; and mutated viruses can be crossed one with another. The mutant offspring create proteins different from those of the original viruses. From these processes it is possible to make deductions as to how the genetic code becomes effective during the formation of the protective covering for the virus. As we shall see, this code has not been deciphered by a long way, but a few things are at any rate known with certainty. The individual signals do not blot each other out; that is to say, none of the four bases signals simultaneously the end of one piece of information and the beginning of the next. Meaningless signals are few, whereas the signal for a particular amino acid is repeated very frequently.

The code seems to be universal. It is to be found in the virus just as in plant or animal cells cultivated in culture mediums. The geneticist still does not know for certain whether the alternation of the initials in the order A, G, T, and C has a special meaning or not. The assumption is made, however, that it does. Accordingly asparagine corresponds without doubt to the alternation ACA, glutamine to the combination AAC, and threonine to CAA.

To draw up the genetic formula for a grown man in its entirety would require the deciphering of a million genes, and it should be remembered that up to now no one has ever succeeded in decoding one single gene completely. A huge task has still to be performed. The formula for a man would be composed of 600 million words; it is inscribed in a chromosome fiber fifteen inches in length. Everything is housed in this one formula: brain, nervous system, psyche. Genetics is still ignorant of how the various parts of the code are connected with each other. On the other hand it is already known how the information from the "steps of life" is transmitted to those elements in the cell that build up amino acids and protein out of nourishment.

THE INFORMATION-CARRIERS: RNA

The interior of the cell is not yet so thoroughly researched as the interior of the atom. To understand properly what is going on the biologist needs new instruments that have not yet been invented. The interior of a cell can be regarded as a sun surrounded by satellites, the ribosomes. These satellites swim around in the cell fluid that encircles the nucleus, and are sometimes settled on the inner side of the cell membrane. They are chemical manufacturing plants in miniature, fully automatic to an extent unimaginable for us. They produce to order the most complex chemical combinations in existence: proteins. They receive their orders from ribonucleic acid (RNA), an "information acid" fairly similar to DNA. The one difference is that the "banister" is constructed from a different sugar: RNA employs ribose instead of DNA's deoxyribose. In addition one of the DNA bases, thymine, is replaced in RNA by another base, uracil. RNA is produced by DNA, leaves the nucleus of the cell, travels through the cell fluid to the ribosomes, and there sets in motion the protein synthesis. This process can be followed step by step in the organism.

If living cells are crushed in clay the result is a sugar containing DNA, RNA, ribosomes, and other chemical combinations—in particular enzymes, organic catalysts essential for synthesis. If this mass is placed into a culture medium with amino acids and the phosphate combinations for the supply of the necessary energy, the ribosomes contained in it produce proteins just as though they were in a cell.

Now the amino acids can be marked with radioactive carbon (C^{14}). The order in which they penetrate the protein molecules during the synthesis can then be followed. Adding to the mixture RNA from other organisms (for example, RNA from a virus to an extract taken from bacteria) changes the protein substances formed. If synthetic RNA is injected, instructions can be given to the ribosomes according to which amino acids are then produced. Biology is thus succeeding gradually in assembling the "genetic dictionary" of information acid.

There is no difficulty in deducing the genetic code of DNA from the genetic code of the information acid, and so it is possible to put together the "genetic dictionary" not only of RNA but also of DNA.

The geneticists are succeeding, slowly but surely, in cracking the code; but some of the discoveries are terrifying. For instance, if one single "word" in this code is changed, the result is incurable illness from birth (a well-known example is the bleeding sickness, or hemophilia).

In the hemoglobin of a man suffering from a certain kind of anemia only one single "word" varies from those in the hemoglobin of other people. Normal hemoglobin has glutamic acid at a certain point in the molecule chain, while anemics have valine at the same spot. Glutamic acid and valine are both among the twenty words of the "language of life," the twenty amino acids previously listed. Three letters in the genetic code, one word in the long "sentence" of the hemoglobin different from the norm—and a life is wrecked.

Until 1959 the terrible curse of mongolism was a mystery to scientists and doctors. Mongolism, so called because most children suffering from it have mongoloid features, is an inborn physical and mental stunting of growth that shows itself immediately at birth. Mongoloids attain at most the mental development of a three- or four-year-old child. One out of seven hundred infants is mongoloid. The total number of these unfortunate people on earth must reach approximately one million. The French scholar Turpin and his collaborators Lejeune and Gautier have discovered that mongolism is due to chromosomal aberration. The human cell normally contains forty-six chromosomes; the nuclei of the gametes, or sex cells, each have twenty-three chromosomes, and the uniting of sperm cell and an egg cell brings the count back to forty-six. But the body cells of mongoloids have forty-seven chromosomes. How this forty-seventh chromosome causes mongolism is not known, nor has the discovery of chromosome imbalance as yet led to the development of an effective treatment.

Since this discovery was made and later confirmed by scientists in many countries, it has been possible to trace the cause of many illnesses and anomalies to chromosomal aberration, in particular the Turner syndrome, which is the cause of infertility in women. Lejeune has observed that this illness is caused by the lack of one of the two X (or sex) chromosomes in the nuclei of women. Certain spinal deformities go back to a quite specific chromosomal aberration: one small chromosome sticks to another, which then declines and decays. In this case the patient has a chromosome count of only forty-five.

GENESIS OF A LIVING BEING

We are gradually beginning to understand our own genesis. A mysterious force collects atoms along the threads formed by the chromosomes. The filaments split longitudinally, separate, and pass to the ribosomes, ordering them to form proteins from the amino acid taken up through the medium or built on the spot. The proteins are compounded from the atoms and molecules of the amino acids and from energy usually supplied by molecules containing phosphates—all protein substances, for nails and hair as well as for the brain. The amino acids are controlled by RNA, which arranges them in such a way that the requisite quantity of protein results.

The chemical processes under discussion here are of unimaginable complexity. Every single reaction is programmed and controlled.

Everything—hair, eyes, intelligence, character—is realized according to programming older than time. It may be conceivable that we can later change ourselves by sheer will power, and perhaps our environment will have modifying effects—but what we are at birth is programmed with 600 million "words" on a fifteen-inch-long chromosome filament of DNA. To be able to change the hereditary mass we must know what these "words" are. For twenty years now we have had at least some idea. But we are still far from being in a position to transcribe the program of heredity as we transcribe magnetic tape. This transcription may however one day be within our capabilities if the French scientists Sadron, Douzon, and Polowsky, together with the Russian Blumenfeld, are right and the acids of the genetic code are magnetic. Once this hypothesis has become a certainty we will be able to record the genetic formulae of all living beings on magnetic tapes. We will then perhaps discover unsuspected relationships—the history of evolution will no longer be a mystery.

We will also know then why the cancer cell has a different genetic makeup than the healthy cell, and it may be possible for us to modify this makeup in such a way that the cancered cell will heal itself.

DARING VISIONS: CHANGING THE HEREDITARY MASS

Even such a method of healing cancer would be a near miracle. But that would only be the beginning. The realization of all that nature has not created because it didn't want to or because Lady Luck was not standing by would become conceivable. One day perhaps it will be possible to inoculate the nuclei of a horse with data from the nuclei of a bird to program the birth of horses with wings. In this way the geneticist would create a real Pegasus. Even more bizarre combinations are conceivable, as illustrated by some geneticists' jokes: a crossing of the pigeon and the parrot, to arrange for the oral communication of messages; a crossing of the fly and the glowworm, so that you can swat troublesome flies in the dark; a crossing of the cow and the giraffe, so that the animal can graze on your neighbor's field but be milked on your own.

Geneticists may well succeed in modifying the genes of a plant in such a way that it produces aspirin, or in carrying out changes in the hereditary mass of a cow to ensure that its milk will contain antibiotics. Mammals may be created that are capable of living in thin mountain air or even on other planets. However, these visions of the genetic possibilities of the future are amusing only so long as man remembers that he is himself of flesh and blood and therefore subject equally to modification.

Einstein was the first to say, "I do not believe in upbringing. Every individual must be his own image, even if the image is a terrible one." A prophetic, frightening statement, for we are on the threshold of an age in which man will be capable of effecting changes in man. In view of mankind's present stage of consciousness, the fear must remain that mutations will be made to serve mediocre aims rather than high ideals. Governments that need men may take care to provide for the birth of more boys than girls. And it is to be feared that they may arrange to have easily influenced slaves produced. It is also to be feared that special value will be ascribed to the production of human beings programmed to be immune to radioactive radiation, even if this programming means the displacement or leaving out of other, more valuable properties. We will have to be prepared for the worst if molecular biology, which is infinitely more dangerous than nuclear physics, is not made subject to controls. Never before has mankind been under such threat from science. But science has never before opened up to mankind possibilities of such magnitude.

CONTINUING EVOLUTION

The first grunting prehistoric men could not foresee language and music. We are equally in the dark about what will happen once we understand the genetic code and are in a position to alter it. The first thought that occurs is that man will place himself on the next step up in the evolutionary process, and create superman. Certain powerful poisons, radioactive rays, and other factors that we do not yet know rip out the "steps" from the spiral staircase of life and put them back in a different order. Most of these changes do not correspond to information supplied by the genetic code. The living organism brought into being by mutation is either incapable of survival or sterile. But occasionally it happens that a mutation stays and the changed living organism steps up to a higher level on the journey of everything alive into the infinite. Man himself evolved in this way.

Today no scientist would deny the evolution of living organisms. But how to explain this evolution of such unimaginable breadth and scope? Lamarck believes that organic structures are subject to self-mutation through usage and that adaptation to the surroundings is the basic premise of evolution. According to Darwin, individuals of the same species differ, and the most successfully adapted survive the struggle for existence and reproduce by natural selection (survival of the fittest). Both hypotheses are not completely in accord with what we know today about the mechanism of heredity. Geneticists incline today to the surmise that the mutant genes at the time of the genesis of living organisms were different from those of today.

IS MAN THE HIGHEST FORM OF EVOLUTION?

With what were these mutant genes in communication? With different conditions of life on our planet? With different cosmic radiations? When we look at the world around us and at man himself, we get the impression that life is frozen and evolution at a standstill. Is man the climax and conclusion of evolution? Or can he himself cause the creation of the superman? Once the genetic code is deciphered the geneticist will know the combinations for intelligence, equilibrium of the nervous system, resistance to high-speed acceleration (especially important for interplanetary flights), and even parapsychological capabilities. But the further development of these properties signifies only a quantitative improvement of what man already possesses. To create a living organism qualitatively different from man of today it would be necessary to construct spiral staircases of life from other letters different from the four that comprise the genetic code. Different bases would have to be used, and combinations of atoms other than adenine, guanine, cytosine, and thymine. Chemistry already is able to manufacture synthetic bases by the million. But how can it be foreseen whether the introduction of Base X into the spiral will perhaps lead to properties or capabilities just as unimaginable to us as a nuclear reactor would have been to Neanderthal man? A solution to this problem—to my knowledge the only one hitherto proposed— has been put forward by the science-fiction fiction author Jack Williamson in his book *Dragons' Teeth*. His solution takes us to the borders of human imagination. Williamson believes that the human mind can have direct influence on matter; he calls this capacity psychokinetics. Some parapsychologists, Rhine and Thorwald for instance, claim to have established experimentally the existence of such a capacity, but their results are not convincing. Williamson makes use of his privilege as a novelist and allows his imagination free play. He is convinced that psychokinetics is the most effective means of achieving mutations. In his opinion the human will, together with the forces of the subconscious, can influence the genes and so rearrange the molecules that an evolution to the superman can oe set in motion. There is nothing, however, as yet to prove that we will ever possess such powers. If we are to remain on the more certain foundations of science, then in what way would a control over the genetic code be conceivable? Mathematics is an important aid here.

WITH THE AID OF MATHEMATICS

Mathematics will help us to analyze the data of a genetic message. It will also show us how a genetic message may be so enriched that it becomes not only more complex but also more beautiful. The concept of beauty in mathematics, especially in applied mathematics, will then attain its full significance. Every possible genetic code is a raw mass, a manifestation that can be analyzed. Already mathematical formulas have been developed to correspond to artistic or musical beauty. The combination of the human mind and the capacities of highly developed electronic computers will certainly make possible the discovery of formulas corresponding to genetic beauty. When that happens man will be able to influence the genetic code in such a way that living organisms are created that are more beautiful than we are. The first of these new living organisms, equipped with capacities of mind which we neither possess nor can even imagine, will take up once again the flame of evolution and continue the climb of the living organism into the eternal.

—Jacques Bergier

Man and the Universe

The official scientific milestones of 1963 were the genetic code and the Mars and Venus satellites. But a number of other things happened that year; although they received less public limelight—indeed were hardly taken notice of by the press—nonetheless they were of the highest significance.

MICRO-ORGANISMS 250 MILLION YEARS OLD

In first place the "rediscovery" of Paleozoic algae must be mentioned. The Tass news agency reported comprehensively the strange discoveries made by N. T. Tchudinov in the salt mines at Beresniki in the Ural mountains: ordinary cooking salt (or sodium chloride), magnesium chloride (from which a metal important for aviation can be extracted), and calcium chloride (which is used for making artificial manure) in sedimentary beds laid down in the Paleozoic Era—which means 250 million years ago. In 1956 Tchudinov began examining these salts. His aim was to discover why cooking salt is colorless while the other two salts have various colorations. The research also had a practical purpose: knowledge of what causes the coloration would make it easier to establish the best technique to use for compounding the various salts.

At that time the surmise was general that the coloration was due to infiltrating iron oxide. And in fact Tchudinov's first experiments showed that the salt pollutants contained a lot of iron. But other elements were also present, notably carbon. Continuing his experiments, Tchudinov established that the colored salts all contained almost 1 per cent of organic matter. Which meant that the salt mine was composed of organic matter to the tune of some 100 million tons!

For what reason did these tiny colored crystals contain so high a content of organic materials?

One day Tchudinov noticed that they underwent a strange transformation in a solution of sodium chloride. They opened up and formed a greenish-yellow substance, in the interior of which small green nuclei could be seen. Finally a regular bud evolved, out of which came a species of algae.

Tchudinov repeated the experiment countless times. On almost every occasion he obtained the same result. The colored crystals were transformed into living substance. For advice he turned first of all to scientists in the area, then to experts in biology and palaeontology in Leningrad and Moscow. They all put the same question: Are the microorganisms under discussion recent or ancient? There was only one way to answer this question and that was to repeat the experiment a great many times, taking utmost care to prevent the infiltration of microorganisms from the immediate environment. That was done.

After countless experiments even the most skeptical of the experts had to agree that it was a case of algae that had slumbered for 250 million years.

Similar discoveries have been made in recent years. H. J. Dombrowski succeeded in Germany in reviving bacteria found in the salt mines at Zechstein. The salt strata date back 180 million years. However, the experiments by Dombrowski and his colleagues yielded only a very few microorganisms. Tchudinov's experiments were the first to open up to our gaze a significant mass of slumbering living organisms to the exclusion of all possibility of error, thanks to countless repetitions of the experiments. It should be noted that both in Beresniki and in Zechstein the microorganisms were protected from destructive cosmic rays by a layer of sediment several hundred meters thick. This is of crucial importance; the intensity of cosmic radiation underneath such a protective layer of sediment is very low.

TO OTHER PLANETARY SYSTEMS

Another extraordinary report emanated from the United States. It concerned the technique worked out by Stanley Leinwoll following research work by Roy Nelson to discover planets that revolve around different suns from ours. The report was published in the April 1963 issue of the periodical *Analog*.

In brief, the essentials of the discovery: Roy Nelson, long-distance communications specialist for RCA, demonstrated in 1954 that the solar eruptions that interfere with communications take place especially when the planets Jupiter and Saturn are in a certain position relative to the sun, in particular when they are at angles of 0, 90, 180, or 270 degrees to the sun. Subsequently, statistical calculations have established similar effects between the earth, Venus, and Mars. It is by no means a case here of astrological speculation. The truth is rather that there is quite simply a periodicity which is indicated by the planets. It can be explained by the tendency to retain certain angles. The interferences are caused by the gravitation of the particular planet affecting the sun at a given moment. Leinwoll then undertook the investigation of other suns outside our solar system to see whether similar disturbances, or eruptions, could be tracked and recorded there. If there were such eruptions, then the conclusion could be drawn that the suns in question are orbited by planets. Sophistication of the research techniques made it possible to establish the existence of small planets no bigger than the earth, Mars, or Venus. According to Leinwoll our galaxy has 10 million inhabited planets. Radio astronomers are at present using the Leinwoll techniques to observe and analyze Tau Ceti, a size-four star eleven light-years from the earth and probably orbited by planets. It is hoped that definite knowledge will be forthcoming soon.

THE PLACE OF MAN IN THE UNIVERSE

The researches of Tchudinov and Leinwoll, the deciphering of the genetic code, and man's explorations in space all have one thing in common. They are all inspired by the same questions: Where does life come from? When did it start? When will it stop? Men of all times have put these questions. In our time, with the prospect opened up by the advances in science and technology that they might one day be answered, they have become more urgent. Behind the effort to discover whether other suns are also orbited by planets is the question of whether these planets can one day accommodate forms of life. The most important question of our times concerns the place of man—or rather of his intelligence—in the womb of the universe. For that reason, one of the most significant scientific triumphs of recent years was the discovery by the Americans Claus and Nagy of microorganisms in carbon meteorites. The salt-mine researches of the Russians aroused such wide interest because they proved once again how resilient and enduring life is.

—Jacques Bergier

Life Out of a Test Tube

Starting from a few experiments in their own hearths, the race of chemists have built up a quite fantastic philosophy.

—Francis Bacon

SCIENCE'S GREATEST ADVENTURE

Modern science has set itself the task of awakening inanimate matter to life and creating life synthetically. When we speak of this bold endeavor of science, it must first of all be made clear that the life being talked about is life as we know it on this planet, that is to say, living organisms constructed of cells. The research underway at many institutions has a very precise purpose: to create living cells synthetically. There is no thought at the present time of fabricating microbes or rabbits, apes or men. Once a living cell has been successfully put together, it will need an evolution spanning 3 billion years to progress from a single-cell organism to a man. But even the creation of a cell would be an extremely significant milestone in the history of organic chemistry.

The difficulties of the undertaking are enormous, and yet they seem smaller today than ten years ago. To set in motion the formation of cells it would presumably be enough to synthesize the acids of the nuclei in the interior of the cells, then expose them to an appropriate environment. This environment would have to correspond to the earth's atmosphere 3 billion years ago. Scientists can only surmise what the atmosphere was like in those days. It is assumed that it was a mixture of methane, ammonia, and steam. In those days there was no oxygen and no carbon dioxide.

Scientists today want to generate life in such an artificially created atmosphere. They hope to be successful in manufacturing nucleic acids very similar at least to those in the cell nucleus. These nucleic acids have the property of self-reproduction, but more important, they organize the surrounding matter.

To achieve a synthesis of this kind scientists have used electrical discharges, radiation, and chemical catalysts. Chance plays a very large part. Never has the adventure of science been so poetic. Never has so much scope been given to the imagination. Intuition and daring have never been so important. Yet the scientists, out to discover the still-unknown origins of life, must never lose sight of realities. They do not not know for sure what factors played a part in the origin or origins of life on our planet. Probably that will never be known.

THE EARTH'S ATMOSPHERE BEFORE
THE GENESIS OF LIFE

All that is needed is to find a single way to move from the extremely simple inorganic water, methane, and ammonia molecules to the spiral-shaped, organic, giant molecules of RNA and DNA. Ordinary organic chemistry seems incapable of bringing about such syntheses. For that reason new possibilities have been tried. We would like to describe a few of the successful experiments.

Stanley Miller, while a student at Columbia University, had the brilliant idea of transmitting a high-frequency current of 60,000 volts through a mixture of ammonia, hydrogen, steam, and methane. He used simple apparatus of the sort that could have been used to set up the experiment in the nineteenth century. But nobody thought of it then.

After the charge the mixture was changed. Relative to the exact components of the experiment between 3 and 15 per cent of the mixture had been transformed into complex organic combinations, the names of which we list here, since they document an important conquest of modern chemistry: glycine, alanine, glutamic acid, sarcosine, beta-alanine, alpha-amino-butylic acid, N-methylanine, aspartic acid, amino diacetic acid, amino acetopropriomic acid, ants' acid, acetone acid, propriomic acid, glucol acid, tartaric acid, alpha-hydro-butylic acid, succic acid, carbamic acid, methyl carbamic acid.

All these chemical compounds are organic in nature, and are therefore usually created by living organisms. A few of them have been for some time capable of synthetic manufacture, like carbamic acid and ants' acid, but others, especially glycine and alanine, are complex organic metabolism products. Like Pasteur's colleagues, Miller's colleagues raised all conceivable objections. It was pointed out that living organisms can only be generated by living organisms, and that was true also for complex organic compounds; therefore the organic compounds created in the experiments must have been generated by microorganisms. Miller sterilized his apparatus for 18 hours at 130° C., then repeated his experiment. He got the same results. Today nobody doubts the accuracy of his claims: amino acids can be constructed by massive electrical discharges through elementary gases. Other reactions, still not proven but under research, make possible, as we will see, the construction of nucleic acids from amino acids.

WHEN HYDROGEN EVAPORATES

Dr. Cyril Ponnamperuma is from Ceylon; today he works at the famous Lawrence Laboratory at the University of California. In June 1963 he bombarded an artificial "prehistoric atmosphere" created out of methane, ammonia, and steam with rapid electrons for forty-five minutes. The result exceeded all the scientist's expectations. Among the end products was an entire step of the spiral staircase of life, adenine.

This is the most complex compound man has so far been able to manufacture in the laboratory. This advance encourages great hopes. If it is possible to synthesize one of the steps of the spiral staircase of life, then why not also the three other steps, and subsequently the entire chromosome spiral?

The scientist from Ceylon tested his experiment with great care and changed the conditions of the experiment. He observed that noticeably less adenine was formed if hydrogen was added to the starting mixture. The conclusion can be drawn that life could only manifest itself on earth after hydrogen, one of the principal components of prehistoric atmosphere, had evaporated into interplanetary space. Hydrogen cannot be held by the earth's gravity because the gravitational pull is too weak for so light a gas, and so it drifted away from our planet. Subsequently the influence of cosmic and solar radiation—in all probability—caused the genesis of life under conditions that Miller and Ponnamperuma have reconstructed in miniature.

THE KNOWLEDGE OF THE ALCHEMISTS

The second sensational piece of news traveled around the world just a few years ago. Gerhard Schramm, a well-known German biochemist at the Max Planck Institute in Tübingen, manufactured a compound that contained amino acids and saccharides. In keeping with the ancient hermetic tradition and the ideas of Paracelsus he added phosphate to the compound, the element which the alchemists believed to contain the secret of life. Schramm did not, it is true, take pure phosphoric acid but rather an organic polyphosphate, a compound of linear and cyclical ethers in phosphoric acid. When he heated the compound to approximately 60° C. he achieved chemical compounds with a molecular weight of up to 50,000! Water has a molecular weight of 18, DNA and RNA of approximately 1 million. The acids created by Schramm behaved in addition like genuine nucleic acids. Observed under an electron microscope, spirals and ropelike structures can be picked out. At the same time the scientist observed how saccharides with a molecular weight of up to 40,000 were created that were very similar to the saccharines existing in the RNA and DNA spirals. Schramm's nucleic acids consist of up to 150 "chain links." Under the electronic microscope their resemblance to DNA and RNA is astonishing. They may have only 150 "limbs," but the tobacco virus has only 6000. The difference is not all that great.

THE CHAIN OF LIFE

The alchemists already knew that to penetrate the secret of life and to progress from the amino acids to the nucleic acids, phosphate was necessary. How did they come into possession of this key to the world of living organisms? We do not yet know the answer to this question, but it is entirely possible that traces of a truly ancient culture may one day be found in alchemy.

The molecular weight of the tiniest viruses is around 10 million. To get there from methane, ammonia, and water, the following path is perhaps taken:

First Step: Amino acids are formed by electrical charges, bombardments by electrons, or suitable radiation.

Second Step: The amino acids are converted to nucleic acids, using polyphosphates as catalysts.

Third Step: Using appropriate catalysts that have still to be found, the spiral-shaped molecules of the nucleic acids are allowed to form a culture medium in which a virus can be formed. The first virus to be formed in this way will presumably be different from the viruses we already know. All living organisms, especially men, must be protected against any contact with this virus, since it could cause a new disease against which we have no protection. On the other hand it is to be hoped that among the artificially synthesized viruses there may be one or several dangerous to cancer cells but not to normal cells. In such an event the synthesis of life would have made a direct contribution to the advancement of medicine. But the theoretical consequences of such a successful synthesis would be far more significant than the practical applications.

GENERATING LIFE IN ORDER TO UNDERSTAND IT

There are numerous aspects of life that cannot be analyzed. The specific properties of the cell will be capable of complete elucidation only by a synthesis. The course of chemical and physical processes is not the same inside the cell as it is outside. Life uses the catalyst in a very imaginative way fundamentally different from its use in chemistry.

It was probably many millions of years before such perfection was attained. Professor J. D. Bernal, who teaches crystallography at Birkbeck College, University of London, formulates it this way:

As long as there were only tiny molecules formed by the condensation of carbon monoxide and ammonia, nothing could exist which resembles an individualized organism; there were at best small zones in which the compound remained more constant and in which a metabolism took place during a certain time, but that something was more akin to cold light than to organisms as we know them today. All these subvital units were fairly similar to each other, even if they were not alike; their outer limits were probably only weakly formed and variable, and they were able to melt into each other or join with each other without complication. If two were not compatible, one or both were destroyed; but if they were compatible the compounding resulted in an extension of the scope of their biochemical activities. Gradually this process had to lead, through a sort of natural selection, to better functioning and to a unity within the regions in which the exchange was possible and which—for instance in the case of large marshes—could cover an area of several square miles.

Life generated artificially in the laboratory will skip over this phase of cold light and progress directly to the stage of the virus or even the small bacteria. The transformation will be tracked step by step so that the whole process can be understood.

To return to the practical applications: a consequence to look forward to one day will be the ability of industry to manufacture saccharides and fats out of air. The problem of hunger in the world would then be solved. But still more exciting would be the artificial synthesis, in the laboratory, of purely spiritual life.

It is surmised that the synthetically generated DNAs and RNAs will somehow be successful in extracting from an appropriate culture medium the elements of a cell with which they surround themselves, and most importantly a cell membrane, which seals off every cell from the world. This surmise is not proven and not yet provable, yet it is subscribed to by virtually all scientists. No one of course has the slightest idea how this miracle will actually happen in all its detail. The one certainty is that the questions that will be asked and the answers that will be given will fill a row of thick volumes.

RETURN TO LOUIS PASTEUR

Even as late as the middle of this century, if discussion had turned to the artificial generation of life, all chemists would have declared such a synthesis to be unrealizable for reasons of symmetry. Pasteur had demonstrated that chemical substances synthetically generated tend to have a double action optically; that is to say, they are a compound of two substances, one of which turns the polarization level of light to the right, the other to the left. Substances generated by living organisms on the other hand are optically single-visioned, and turn their polarization axis therefore exclusively to the left or the right. At the time of Pasteur and for a long time after him there was no way known to separate a substance with double vision into two substances with single vision.

Pasteur was of the opinion that such a separation remained God's privilege and would never be accorded to man, unless he split crystals by hand under the microscope, which in turn would once again represent an interference with life. Later a separation procedure was developed by which one of the components was consumed by a certain kind of microbe. Here again life was a factor. Today the opinion is held that the difficulties are not so insuperable as Pasteur and his followers thought. Asymmetrical substances have been generated without invasion by a living organism. The sun's corona and the moon transmit polarized light to us, and its influence over millions of years has led to the formation of polarized substances. The magnetic field of the earth plays a part too in this polarization. If the chemist succeeds in generating optically double-visioned substances, he will be in a position to create the asymmetry necessary for living organisms, by using polarized light of sufficient power.

In 1945 Tenney and Ackerman succeeded in creating, with the aid of circular polarized light, an optically single-visioned acetic acid. In 1953 the Frenchman Darmois postulated a general method of separating an optically double-visioned compound into its two optically single-visioned components by successive crystallization. Pasteur's objection is no longer valid today.

LIVING ORGANISMS IN THE ANTIPODE WORLD

Meanwhile a highly interesting problem suggests itself. If a virus is created synthetically, then brought into life by separating it into two parts which are, as it were, image and reflection, then in actual fact not one but two lives have been generated: one life of earthly type and one life that is the anti-image of life on earth in the world behind the mirror, exisiting somewhere in the antipode world.

Not long ago the Chinese-American scientists Lee and Yang demonstrated through experiments with elemental particles that space is not symmetrical in our region of the universe, and that the tiniest particles have a tendency to spin around their own axis in a certain direction. This phenomenon has been designated as the invalidation of the law of parity. It is not yet known how this phenomenon links up with the symmetry essential for living matter; but if a different universe exists, then life there is presumably the antithesis to life in our world.

The possibility exists therefore that chemical synthesis generates simultaneously two kinds of life, two kinds of viruses or microbes. The one corresponds to our region of the universe, the other corresponds to living organisms in the antithetical world. This second kind of life would presumably have to be fed on asymmetrical products manufactured specially. The problem of symmetry will perhaps be illuminated a little in this way.

The problem interested Curie more than did radioactivity, and Pasteur found it more fascinating than microbes. Geometry applied to chemistry and biology has rendered some truly strange results. If the object could be rotated in a fourth dimension, then a crystal rotating to the right could be transformed into a crystal rotating to the left, or a living organism of this world could be transormed into a living organism of the antithetical world.

In the same manner this process could—if realizable—make a left shoe into a right shoe and a right shoe into a left shoe. A man who had gone through the process would have his heart on his right side. This theme is the subject of H. G. Wells's "The Plattner Story." An explosion accidentally propels the hero into rotation in the fourth dimension, after which he returns to earth. The story was written in 1897, yet even then Wells wrote: "His heart is probably on the right, but that will be established for sure only at the autopsy, because nobody can guess what goes on in the recesses of the human body." In the same year Rontgen discovered the X-rays named after him in some countries! Reality succeeds even in exceeding the imagination of an H. G. Wells.

Will the synthesis of living organisms help us to explore the secrets of the fourth dimension? If man generates simultaneously two living organisms, one the reflected image of the other, will he be capable of effecting a mutual transformation? In this context such questions suggest themselves with some urgency. Like all great scientific discoveries, the synthesis of life will create more problems than it will solve.

At any rate it seems certain that geometry will play an important part in the formation of the living organisms. Very little is known as yet about the accumulation of the particles, their arrangement in spiral forms, the rotation of the spirals around their own axis, the whole complex architecture of the living organism. Serious scientists are keenly interested in the fabrication of paper cutouts in order to find out how folding in right angles could lead to the complex spirals and screws of the nucleic acids.

THE NUMBER FIVE AND LIFE

Water will probably play a part in the synthesis of life. Already it has been shown that water not only is necessary for all living organisms but is also a factor in the crystallization of certain proteins. Perutz and his team have shown that compounding with water molecules plays a decisive part in this process. The quantity of water can vary greatly, but it seems that as a rule the protein molecules are separated by only one or two molecular layers of water. If there are more water molecules, then those that close the gaps between the protein molecules are arranged as in ice. Crystallization is not a common biological phenomenon. Such compounds were probably of only inferior significance at the genesis of life.

Bernal has demonstrated that water as a component of living organisms is organized according to a symmetrical system corresponding to pentagonal solids. Several years ago he demonstrated his point before the British Royal Society. He used a container filled with pentagons and other containers with cubes, prisms, and other solids with fewer or more than five angles. When he tipped over the container with the pentagons, they flowed out and away from each other like a fluid. But the other geometrical solids knocked against each other and therefore did not "flow." This pentagonal organization explains why water flows. The fact that we have five fingers has possibly some cosmic significance. The symmetry of all higher forms of organized life based on water perhaps rests on the number five.

Under the influence of radiation or "contagions" of any kind, or through contact with living organisms, water seems to take on a special form, to become activated. Piccardi has shown that activated water is of the highest importance for the stability of systems of life. It will perhaps be necessary to bring activated water into use at a certain stage in the synthesis of life, probably at the condensation of amino acids to nucleic acids. This transformation can at present be effected by radiation from electromagnetic waves.

SYNTHETIC LIVING ORGANISMS HAVE TO BE STIMULATED INTO LIFE

Viruses, the simplest forms of life, show off two aspects, one crystalline and one living. They form therewith the frontier of life. The great French scientist René Berthélemy, one of the inventors of television, wrote just a few hours before his death: "In a few hours, perhaps in a few minutes, I shall have crossed the threshold which separates the living molecule from the crystal." Viruses bestraddle this threshold. The first synthetic viruses in crystalline form will probably die out of the proper environment. Then it will be necessary to awaken them to life. This presents an enormous problem that most writers on the synthesis of life have obviously seen mistakenly. Presumably the synthetic organism can be stimulated into life by receiving some appropriate living nourishment, for instance a tobacco leaf, since the tobacco virus, one of the most thoroughly researched viruses, progresses from the crystalline to the living state inside such a leaf. Or perhaps vivification can be achieved through appropriate radiation or by bombardment with elemental particles.

Modern science is undeniably close to a synthesis of life. But it could just as well be twenty years as six months before the synthesis is successfully accomplished; it will not in my opinion be much longer. Will man then be able to progress from the synthetic virus to more complex cells, to synthetic multiple cells? I do not think so. In my opinion a complex living organism is composed not only of matter but also of 3 billion years of time. It is the tip of an evolution that has proceeded over a definite period of time, and it cannot be reproduced in a single moment. But even the synthetic generation of a virus would represent the crowning moment of our scientifically oriented culture and would mark the beginning of a new era in biology.

—Jacques Bergier

Anti-Matter:
A Scientific Fact

*Matter has presumably thousands more
properties which we do not know.*

—Voltaire

PARALLEL WORLDS

It is talked about the way nuclear fission was talked about in 1938. Reports by political refugees, hints by scientists or politicians, science-fiction stories—all are creating an atmosphere similar to the one in which the world first began to believe in the possibility of an atom bomb. There is talk of weapons more destructive than anything ever deployed, indeed than anything in the secret arsenals of the military powers. There is talk of interstellar rockets powered by the total destruction of matter—and of catastrophes that have already occurred in the laboratories of some researchers.

A recent memorandum signed by seventeen prominent American scientists pointed out that the United States has fallen behind considerably in the area of anti-matter research. Simultaneously the Soviet press accused the Americans of wanting to create the "ultimate weapon" that would make possible the destruction of entire continents. In France science buries its head in the sand and claims simply that there is no such thing as anti-matter.

Is anti-matter a reality, as is believed in most countries, or a fairy tale, as is thought in France? What part do fantasy and science fiction have in the rumors flying around at the present time?

In 1932 the English Nobel prize winner Paul Dirac postulated a new theory about the electron. According to his calculations, the observable world—atoms, men, stars—is only an extremely thin layer over the surface of the true reality. This true reality is an ocean compounded of elemental particles. It is unimaginably dense. The particles of which it is compounded are, in contrast to our observable

135

world, in a state in which their energy is smaller than zero: their energy is negative. This ultimate reality, the Dirac Ocean, cannot be perceived by us. But cosmic radiation or superenergized particles generated in atom smashers can at least provide some conception of it.

ELECTRON AND POSITRON

Imagine a raft floating on the sea. There is a pipeline from the raft into the water. The pipeline is attached to a pump. once the pump is activated, it is possible to see water flowing on or even above the surface of the sea that was not there before. At the same time air bubbles form in the stream of water, because a pump is never completely water- and airtight. When a drop of water collides with an airbubble it fills it up, both disappear, and once again we see before our eyes the smooth surface of the water. In the same way elemental particles and natural or artificial rays can snatch newly created particles out of the Dirac Ocean. These are electrons and elemental particles that in reality are only holes in the ocean, but that appear to our senses and measuring instruments as anti-particles: positively charged electrons (electrons are negatively charged), which are destroyed on collision with normal electrons.

This fantastic vision was confirmed by experiments. It was demonstrated that artificially accelerated electrons, cosmic rays, and gamma rays are capable of snatching pairs of elemental particles from the vacuum consisting of one normal electron and one positive electron. The positive electron is called a positron. Electron and positron destroy each other when they collide; energy is thereby released in the form of gamma rays.

About fifteen years ago, with the help of the gigantic atom smasher, anti-protons and later anti-neutrons were successfully extracted from the Dirac Ocean. Gradually the realization has dawned that every elemental particle has its anti-particle. For every elemental particle there is a corresponding "hole" in the Dirac Ocean. On collision with an elemental particle the anti-particle is destroyed, releasing the entire energy mass of the matter. This process seems to be an absolute law. When a scientist discovers a new elemental particle, a corresponding anti-particle is discovered soon afterward.

Up to this point we have kept strictly to the facts. From now on it must be borne in mind that we have moved into the realm of speculation.

FROM ANTI-PARTICLES TO ANTI-MATTER

What is known about the composition of ordinary matter? A positively charged atom of protons and neutrons is orbited by negatively charged electrons arranged along bowl-shaped tracks. The terminology of nuclear physics is frequently imprecise; "bowl-shaped" is intended to convey different levels of energy. The electrons do not therefore orbit the atomic nucleus along definite tracks, like the planets orbit the sun. The expressions "positive" and "negative" refer to the electrical charging. Designating the electricity of the electron as negative and that of the proton as positive has no special significance, and is convenience nomenclature. The terms north and south electricity would have been better, and it would have been equally valid to talk of red and blue electricity. The terminology in use at present is likely to confuse the layman. But to repeat our formulation, even if it would not meet with the approval of nuclear physicists: matter is compounded of positively charged atomic nuclei and the negatively charged electrons that orbit them. On the other hand the energy of atoms, like that of electrons, is positive–whereby the word positive this time has the meaning "more than zero." Atoms and electrons swim on an ocean of particles of negative energy—the word negative means "less than zero." The holes in this negative energy layer appear as anti-particles: positive electrons, negative protons, anti-neutrons, anti-hyperons, anti-sigma particles, anti-psi particles, and so on.

Matter can be formed out of elemental particles. However it should be said that to my knowledge strong hydrogen has never been successfully created by the collision of electron and proton bundles. But when fluid hydrogen is bombarded with neutrons, heavy hydrogen is formed, with a nucleus of one proton and one neutron. The physicist has therefore good reason to believe that by means of a chain reaction of neutrons all elements can be compounded out of a prehistoric state of chaos that contains only protons and neutrons.

Does the same phenomenon exist in the case of the hypothetical anti-matter? Can anti-protons and anti-neutrons compound to atoms orbited by positrons? Can anti-hydrogen, anti-iron, anti-mercury be generated? Do many of the galaxies in the universe consist of anti-matter? Is there an anti-universe, an antithetical world in a different continuum of space and time or even in our own continuum that progresses from the future into the past? These are the questions of great import that science is beginning to put in our time.

A positron or positive electron orbiting an atom compounded of anti-neutrons and anti-protons would emit light, the same light emitted by normal matter. The telescope can therefore be of no use to us in elucidating this particular problem. If there are galaxies of anti-matter, then they emit the same light that comes from ordinary galaxies. But if a galaxy of anti-matter collides with a galaxy of ordinary matter, then matter and anti-matter destroy each other, which leads to a colossal explosion. Stars of anti-matter can fall into a universe of ordinary matter without losing their energy, because the ordinary cosmic matter is automatically destroyed upon contact with the surface.

We therefore do not know for certain whether there is such a thing as anti-matter. But many scientists are convinced that anti-matter must exist for reasons of symmetry. Others believe that the universe is not symmetrical. In this event anti-matter would not exist and anti-particles would simply be isolated phenomena generated locally by heavy bundles of energy; if this view is correct, it tears a huge hole in the particles with negative energy which form the Dirac Ocean. It is a viewpoint defended in particular by one of the fathers of atomic fission, Professor Otto R. Frisch, at present director of the Department of Nuclear Physics at the Cavendish Laboratories in Cambridge, England.

Physicists of equal renown believe, however, that there exists not only a parallel universe of anti-matter but also parallel worlds of ordinary matter, but in other dimensions. Pascual Jordan, for instance, surmises that supernovae originate in other worlds and turn up in our universe without warning.

Whatever the truth may be, the fact is that even if anti-matter does not exist in the universe, that circumstance in itself would be no proof that man could not succeed in creating it artificially. Acetyline and plutonium do not exist in nature, yet that does not prevent man from using acetyline in great quantities in the plastics industry, or from making atomic bombs. The question is therefore a legitimate one as to what will happen if man one day succeeds in creating anti-matter.

THE MOST GIGANTIC ENERGY STORAGE PLANT

To generate 10 tons of anti-matter 10^{14} kilowatts would be needed, as much energy in other words as is consumed in the whole world over an entire decade. The electricity used to drive atom smashers would not be enough by a long way to produce and concentrate locally energy masses of such magnitude; what would be needed would be a completely new nuclear reaction, for instance splitting the atom of a transplutonic element into a normal plutonium atom and an anti-atom. Refugee scientists from the Soviet Union have indicated that such reactions have already been developed there. Such information cannot of course be easily verified.

However, if science were to succeed in generating anti-matter as routinely as acetyline or plutonium are generated today, then the most powerful possible storer of energy would thereby be created, since according to all we know matter is destroyed on collision with anti-matter, and the entire matter converted into energy. One ton of matter and one ton of anti-matter produce together two tons of energy, which is 2×10^{13} kilowatts, or 20 billion kilowatt hours. To prevent the destruction and to conserve the anti-matter, it would have to be contained in a magnetic bottle, that is to say in a magnetic field of a certain shape, as used for instance in plasma experiments. The magnetic bottle on its own, however, would probably not be enough; it would have to be fortified by electrical or electromagnetic fields. This technical problem should not by any means be insoluble. If scientists succeed in manufacturing anti-matter, they will also find a way of conserving it. This is all the more true now that it seems as though the exclusivity principle postulated by Wolfgang Pauli, according to which two elemental particles of one and the same system can never be in precisely the same state, may well be valid. (A short elucidation of Pauli's principle: we know from observation that no two people, animals, or plants are ever exactly alike. Pauli's contention is that this principle holds equally true in the microcosm. In a single atom, therefore, no two electrons could possess precisely the same level of energy, since they would then be identical. That explains the periodicity of elements. If Pauli's principle is valid also for anti-matter, the conservation of anti-matter would be easier than hitherto believed.)

Calculations based on the foregoing thoughts yield the conclusion that every anti-element is capable of destroying only the element that corresponds to it: anti-mercury destroys only mercury but not ordinary iron. The storage of anti-matter would in such an event not present any special problem. Not even a magnetic bottle would be necessary. This kind of discovery is perhaps what American scientists were referring to when "sensational" Russian achievements in the field of anti-matter research were mentioned.

At any rate the latest advances in nuclear physics make it seem thoroughly conceivable that in the foreseeable future methods will be worked out both for the synthetic generation of anti-atoms and for the conservation of anti-matter. It is accordingly very possible that in the near future many nations will dispose of considerable reserves of anti-matter. Man would then enter a new phase, harnessing energies never before dreamed of. What will he do with them?

WITH THE FLYING TORCH TO THE STARS

This question was answered by Professor Stanioyukovitch of Moscow in the following way: mankind will conquer the stars! This scientist and his collaborators in his research institute have formulated plans for a space satellite powered by anti-matter, and have begun the research work necessary for its construction. They have christened their spaceship *The Flying Torch*. In such spaceships, which travel almost at the speed of light, mankind could explore the entire universe, or at least all the heavenly bodies in our galaxy and perhaps other galaxies. *The Flying Torch* is based on the following principle: the greater the velocity of the particles emitted from the engine, the faster the acceleration. Professor Stanioyukovitch has postulated that if a spaceship could be constructed that emitted light instead of burning gases, that is to say a sort of flying torch, it could attain speeds which thanks to the contraction of time resulting from the theory of relativity would permit mankind to travel even to the most distant heavenly bodies.

Early on, however, a significant impediment manifested itself. A mirror never reflects light or other electromagnetic rays one hundred per cent. A tiny portion of the energy is absorbed by the mirror. And through the accumulation of billions and billions of calories even such a tiny portion would be enough to cause a mirror to melt.

Stanioyukovitch and his collaborators have solved this problem. They have demonstrated that there is one instance in which the radiation is reflected one hundred per cent for all practical purposes, the reflector absorbing less than one-billionth of the radiation. That happens when the waves are one-tenth of a millimeter in length, that is to say, in the case of electromagnetic waves on the borderline between radio waves and infrared rays, and when the reflector consists of a thick block of polished copper. Readings of extreme precision have shown that a bundle of rays of the appropriate wavelength and of an intensity five million times that of the sun can be reflected virtually in totality by such a copper mirror.

The second obstacle in the way of *The Flying Torch* is the problem of converting the energy released by the destruction of matter by anti-matter into rays with a wavelength of one-tenth of a millimeter. Stanioyukovitch and his team seem, however, to have solved this problem too. I do not believe that some kind of expedient optimism is at work here.

The third obstacle is cosmic radiation. A spaceship traveling at close to the speed of light will be bombarded with significantly more cosmic rays and particles than a spaceship traveling at eight or ten miles per second, as will be easily appreciated. Since the force of cosmic radiation remains more or less constant throughout the universe, a spaceship traveling at high velocity will be struck by more rays than a spaceship traveling more slowly over the same span of time. The radiation dose would very rapidly be fatal for the occupants of the spaceship. Some kind of equipment is therefore necessary that protects the occupants against the danger from outside. The answer is an artificially generated magnetic protective wall.

The Flying Torch would of course have to be constructed in space and fired in such a way that its beams never reach the earth's surface; otherwise large areas of the earth's surface would be burned or even would melt. In Professor Agrest's opinion tektites were caused by the reactors of such "flying torches" that visited the earth in the distant past or were dispatched into the cosmos by very early cultures who had attained an unimaginably lofty level of evolution. A relatively simple formula can be used to calculate the length of the space journey in the time dimension of the occupants of these flying torches.

Applying the formula to a spaceship that travels half its journey with an acceleration corresponding to the pull of the earth's gravity and the other half braking to the same acceleration rate right up to the moment of arrival, the results are fantastic. The occupants of such a flying torch would notice nothing unusual. Gravity in the spaceship would be the same as on earth. Time would seem to be passing normally and smoothly. Yet within a few years they would have reached the most distant stars. After 21 years (measured in the time of which they are conscious) they would be in the innermost center of our Milky Way, 75,000 light-years from the earth. In 28 years they would be at the constellation of Andromeda, the galaxy nearest to us; its distance is 2,250,000 light-years.

Please note that we are not talking here of science fiction. The formula under discussion has been verified experimentally in the laboratory. Using this formula everyone able to handle logarithmic tables can check our calculations. Mistakes are hardly possible, and all the results obtained on this subject agree. It is therefore important to reflect on the importance of this development for mankind.

The scientists who traveled to the constellation of Andromeda would be returned to earth in 56 years; added to that figure should be the years of their stay on whatever planets they investigated. Let us assume that in all they take 65 years—but that is 65 years measured in *their* time dimension. Back on earth 4,500,000 years have gone by in the meantime. Traveling at a velocity close to the speed of light is a conquest not only of space but also of time. Not only the universe but also the future becomes accessible to man. Only science-fiction authors have so far thought of this consequence. But it is now high time that scientists too reflected on the consequences of such an undertaking. Once the travelers are in the future, a return to the past becomes impossible. We are in the real world, not the world of fiction. Wells's time-machine is not realizable and will never be realized. But even the possibility of exploring the universe and returning to earth centuries, thousands of years, or even millions of years later is sufficiently staggering. If, as many believe, history is cyclical, if cultures decline and are reborn, the flying torch could contribute to the conservation of continuity, provide blood transfusions to a declining culture from the bank of a highly evolved science from their past, and also give to it the benefit of all the knowledge collected by the occupants of the spaceship on the planets of other solar systems. Such a colonization not only of space but also of time would be something completely new in the history of mankind. There has been much talk of working for posterity, of preparing a glorious future, of working for the men of the future. The flying torch, the spaceship fueled by anti-matter, would provide us with a real, physical possibility of communicating with posterity. The men of the future will probably undertake journeys into space not only to explore the galaxies but also to communicate to future cultures what they were able to accomplish. This reason alone would make the discovery of anti-matter as significant as the discovery of fire long ago.

THE DARK SIDE OF ANTI-MATTER

Anti-matter promises blessings, but also dangers. An anti-matter bomb, fifty or seventy-five times more powerful than the hydrogen bomb, with a destructive power equal to one to five thousand megatons, could mean the end of our culture. A bomb of this type exploded at great altitude (the technical side of this problem has been studied by the French military technician Camille Rougeron) would set on fire all America or the whole of Europe. An area the size of the United States or the Common Market countries would be completely destroyed by fire. That would be a truly apocalyptic conflagration, a Hiroshima multiplied one hundred thousand times.

One can understand the terror behind Khrushchev's statement that he trembled to think of the possible contents of a scientist's briefcase.

Once there is a store of anti-matter and man is capable of conserving it—anti-matter is not radioactive and in principle may be conserved for an unlimited period—it would not be especially difficult for technologists to develop an anti-matter bomb. All that would be necessary would be the fusion of matter and anti-matter of the same order, and the result would be an explosion of unimaginable magnitude.

Will we one day have to face the news that some country or other has launched into orbit around the earth satellites stocked with anti-matter bombs that can be triggered at any time over any place by means of a radio signal? The seventeen American scientists who signed the manifesto mentioned earlier are afraid of precisely this development. Nobel prize winner Linus Pauling harbors the same fear. When the prize was awarded to him for the second time (the first time he received the Nobel Prize for Chemistry, later the Nobel Prize for Peace), he spoke of bombs in the process of being built that were worse than the atom bomb. He asked for immediate intervention by the United Nations. The present threat is the anti-matter bomb, "a cloud no bigger than a man's hand." When will this threat become a reality? That is difficult to say, but it could be soon.

ANTI-MATTER AND SCIENCE

Anti-matter is therefore a blessing in the eyes of the space technologists and a threat when the military technologists turn their attentions to it. For the research scientist in his laboratory it is a fascinating possibility of breaking through to discoveries as yet undreamed of. One of these discoveries has already been made experimentally by the American Martin Deutsch. He established that the positron and electron, before they destroy each other, join together for a very brief period to form a new compound, positronium.

Inside the positronium molecule the electron and the positron orbit their common center of gravity. The element is lighter than hydrogen—which was formerly thought to be impossible. Positronium is not to be found in the periodic table of the elements. If only there were a way to stabilize it! It evokes dreams of balloons filled with a gas 920 times lighter than hydrogen, of floating metals and aluminums, reminiscent of the floating cities in Swift's *Gulliver's Travels*. Perhaps science will one day be successful in stabilizing positronium, possibly by cooling it to temperatures in the neighborhood of absolute zero, or by sealing it into a structured magnetic field. The study of matter would then be immeasurably enriched.

Positronium is not quite anti-matter, but rather an in-between element on the borderline between two worlds. If anti-matter can be successfully produced, it will perhaps be possible to generate matter with two atoms, one positive and one negative atom—elements that would not fit into any periodic table. Electrons and positrons would orbit this double nucleus on tracks that would never cross.

Anti-matter would make possible still more unusual researches.

An experiment conducted in 1957 at Columbia University by the Chinese-American physicist Mrs. Wu caused an uproar in the scientific world. She succeeded in freezing radioactive cobalt. The frozen cobalt should in theory have emitted electrons symmetrically in all directions. But the experiment showed that the electrons when emitted followed the north-pole path of an electronic magnet used to set them in motion. This astonishing result proved that matter is not symmetrical, as two other Chinese-American scientists, T. D. Lee and C. N. Yang, had postulated as their theory. In other words, the laws of nature change when one moves into a universe symmetrical with our own. The laws of nature of the universe reflected in a mirror are not the same as ours.

This theory was one of the most fantastic ever postulated. It leads to the claim that matter right down to its tiniest particles and space are not symmetrical. According to this theory the universe in which we live is not the universe of the mathematicians, and is not only not Euclidean, but is even spiraled. In everyday reality not only would parallel lines meet, but objects would no longer be the same if they made a journey through space and returned to their starting points.

Since there are two kinds of spiraling in the universe, the temptation has been to assume that our matter spirals in one direction and anti-matter in the other direction, for example one to the right and the other to the left.

The great Soviet physicist Lev Landau, a Nobel prize winner, has demonstrated by calculations that this does indeed seem to be the case. He calls it the principle of absolute symmetry. Since then every

physicist in the world has been dreaming of producing anti-radio cobalt
and thereby repeating the experiment of Mrs. Wu. If the positrons
emitted by the anti-cobalt nucleus were also asymmetrical, then the
theory of absolute symmetry would be proved. In the Netherlands
experiments were made with ordinary matter that emitted positrons.
These experiments indicate that Landau was right. But only an
experiment with anti-radio cobalt would really be conclusive.

AS FAR AS THE MIND CAN REACH

If the theory of absolute symmetry turned out to be correct, it would
have consequences beyond the scope of even the wildest fantasy.
Einstein has shown that space and time cannot be separated. If space is
spiraled, then time can no longer exist either. If the principle of
parity—*i.e.,* of the symmetry of space—breaks down, then the
principle of symmetry between past and future is no longer valid. The
relativity of time was up to now one of the essential fundaments of
physics. According to the theory of relativity the past of one observer
was the future of another, corresponding to their position in space and
their velocity. If this relativity of past and future is taken away from
the physicist, he will draw extremely disturbing conclusions. If time in
the real world is entangled, if the future differs from the past even in
the tiniest particles, if time is composed not out of moments but out of
arrows all pointing to one and the same horizon, or at least in one and
the same world—then physics in its entirety would have to be
rediscovered.

A Russian, Nikolai Alexandrovitch Kosyrev, has had the courage to
tackle this problem. He is a theoretician who has been under heavy
criticism from Soviet scientists. Like many geniuses working purely
intuitively, Kosyrev is less interested in convincing than in showing,
and his proofs lack scientific exactitude. He might even be called a
Sunday mathematician. He is in fact not really a professional
theoretical physicist, but an astronomer who has made valuable
discoveries in his own field. He was the first for instance to observe
northern lights on Venus and streams of burning gas in the Alfons
crater on the moon. Nobody doubts Kosyrev's merits and qualities as
an astronomer. But his new physics, going beyond Einstein and with

time composed of arrows, has still not met with general acceptance. This new physics draws the conclusion that science will one day be capable of extracting energy from the passage of time just as today energy is extracted from flowing water. Kosyrev's theory takes us to the outer limits of the mind. To confirm it laboratory experiments would have to be undertaken with radioactive elements composed of anti-matter. And once confirmed it would take bold spirits to draw from the theory the practical consequences. If time is in fact a stream of whirlpools, if the direction of its current is marked by arrows "stuck" on to the tiniest particles of matter and anti-matter—will it then be possible one day to erect dams to capture the energy of time? With this vision of the future we would like to conclude our excursion into the realm of anti-matter.

—Jacques Bergier

Magic and Science

There is a time for everything.
There is even a time for the reunion of times.
—Louis Pauwels

FACTS AND NOTHING BUT FACTS

The claim that before our scientific age men had already discovered highly developed technologies and found astonishing methods of influencing nature and life is too shocking to be accepted without substantial proofs.

All rational minds—and we count ourselves among their number—are convinced that experiment and calculation are the only source of knowledge. Indeed, once this source is removed the only alternative would seem to be revelation. Even if this expression is not used in its narrower religious sense but rather quite generally, it is nevertheless inhibited by all the threats that hung over the freedom of research up to the liberation of science in the age of the Renaissance and especially in the eighteenth century.

In the retinue of revelation were superstition, esoteric obscurantism, and spiritual tyranny. For when knowledge is afforded by revelation, those chosen for the revelation have the right to impose the truth upon others—sometimes by force.

Today nobody believes in the theory of revelation. Even religiously oriented persons demand freedom in the realm of the sciences. The Dominican physicist Dubarle, for instance, recently stated in public that science had to be materialistic. But if there are no other sources of knowledge than experiment and calculation, is it necessary to consider the accumulated knowledge inherited from lost cultures as of no value? Were there not highly developed cultures before the early advanced cultures known to us?

Research undertaken without prejudice into the cultures that existed before the scientific age would indeed provide us with information of

149

which our science is still totally ignorant. For more than a decade we have been gathering facts, some of which we collected in the book *The Morning of the Magicians*. Was it our purpose to downgrade our civilization of today? Certainly not. Our intention was rather to provide the stimulus for new research, and show the spiritual unity of men of all races, cultures, and times. We are of the ecumenical spirit.

MAGIC AND PHARMACEUTICS

Systematic research into magic from the perspective of pharmaceutics began in 1926 with an essay that has since become a classic: "Action and Clinical Uses of Ephedrine, an Alkaloid Isolated from the Chinese Drug Ma Huang," by K. K. Chen and C. F. Schmidt. The authors, a Chinese and an American, did not, as was the common practice in those days, simply write off the "magic" potentialities of the Chinese drug ma huang, but instead analyzed the plant. They were able to isolate the alkaloid ephedrine. To their work we owe many stimulants: benzedrine, pervitine, and so on. The student swallowing a stimulant before his examinations probably has no idea that he is following an ancient magical practice.

A few years later American scientists began to study the five-thousand-year-old store of Indian magic potions. They discovered reserpine, from which a number of tranquilizers are manufactured today. In the United States alone, 2 billion dollars is spent annually on tranquilizers. The persons taking these medicines probably have no idea that the main ingredient is a substance once fed to people destined for sacrifice to some god.

Only after this pioneering research was any attempt made to examine seriously the magic recipes of the Middle Ages, which may indeed be able to generate the Witches'-Sabbath visions described in the records of witches' trials.

Here is the recipe for the ointment with which the witches rubbed themselves before going to the Sabbath:

      3 grams oeanthol (extract of a poisonous marsh plant)
    50 grams opium
    30 grams betel
      6 grams tannis-leaf

>   15 grams henbane
>   15 grams belladonna
>   250 grams hashish
>   5 grams blister-fly
>   tragacanth
>   powdered sugar

The pharmaceutical industry is still a long way from having exhausted the riches of the ancient magicians; it seems as though the thaumaturgists of earlier times were far in advance of modern chemical methods. The North American Indians used a contraceptive pill which is absolutely reliable. The Africans knew drugs that permit safe abortion in the second or third month of pregnancy. Certain tribes possess plant extracts that awaken and strengthen the parapsychological capacities.

Animal and plant extracts, magic mixtures, which we have ignored because of our long-drawn-out scorn of the "uncivilized" world, reveal secrets that science is a long way from solving. Frank Belknap Long writes, "Apple, tree, and snake are the symbols of great and terrible secrets."

SMITHS, ALCHEMISTS, MAGICIANS

Magic and metal—two related words, two related realms. We have known only for a short time that alloys were used much earlier than pure metals, and that the use of metals and alloys is much more ancient than commonly assumed until recently. Most of our metallurgical technology originated in magic. In Syria steel was made malleable by pushing a red-hot blade into the body of a living slave. The symbolic meaning of this ritual was supposed to be that the magician had transferred the power of the blood to the blade. Today it is known that the same effect can be obtained by plunging the red-hot blade into water filled with animal skins. The element that causes the effect is animal carbon dioxide. From this process modern metallurgy developed its techniques of nitrifying steel and later the more effective method of bombarding steel with carbon dioxide ions.

The Egyptians were the first to know how to harden copper. But no one knows by what method.

Still more extraordinary was the discovery in China of objects made out of an aluminum alloy. An essay in the *Revue de l'Aluminium* for January 1961, based on an article by the archaeologist Yan Hang in the Chinese periodical *Si Vao*, completely upset all our notions about the history of aluminum. Traditionally it had been believed that aluminum was unknown until the beginning of the nineteenth century. It was supposed to have been discovered by Davy in 1807, and not successfully manufactured in the laboratory until 1827, even then with strong impurities, and it was 1854 before the pure version was successfully compounded with the help of a chemical process. Aluminum "existed" therefore only from that date. Industrial manufacture of aluminum was made possible by the electrolytic processes developed by Héroult and Hall. Mankind was therefore thought to have manufactured aluminum only slightly more than one century ago.

This view had to be revised when objects made of metal were found in a burial ground in Kuang-su in eastern China. They were discovered in the grave of a general who had lived in the Tsin Era (A.D. 250–313), and consisted of various alloys, among them an alloy of copper and aluminum. The objects made out of the aluminum-copper alloy were probably belt-fasteners. They were examined by the chemistry faculty in Nanking, in the physics institute of the Chinese Academy of Sciences, and in the Dunbai Polytechnic. Even with the knowledge we possess today we would not be capable of producing such an alloy. Yet it is difficult to believe that they came about by accident. To create them temperatures of over one thousand degrees centigrade are needed. We have no idea how the Chinese were able to generate such high temperatures. It is difficult to arrive at a satisfactory explanation even if it is assumed that carbon and preheated air were used. The probability is that their aluminum bronze was manufactured according to techniques totally unknown to us. Possibly they were able to melt down the copper at low temperatures using reactions we have not yet discovered.

But that is not the only problem. Without going into the details of alchemy, it should be mentioned here that books on magic contain precise references to: a flexible glass made from a mineral (flexible glass masses can be produced today from various artificial plastics, but we are not able to produce a flexible glass from a mineral); absolutely non-corrosible iron; so hard a steel that it was not affected even by aqua regia (aqua regia is compounded of three parts hydrochloric acid and one part sulphuric acid, and dissolves even gold and platinum); metals phosphorescent in the dark. Orichalk, the metal of the people of Atlantis, is said also to have been phosphorescent. Today no metal is known that is independently phosphorescent in the dark.

MAGIC AND ELECTRICITY

Was the *Bundeslade* of the Jews an electrical condenser? The claim has been made, but there are no proofs. What is certain is that electricity was put to magical use in Persia as early as the era of the Sassanites, that is to say between A.D. 224 and 651. The proof was found in 1936 by Dr. Wilhelm König of the Iraqi State Museum in Baghdad. In Khojut Rabu'a, southwest of Baghdad, he discovered clay vessels about six inches tall with a diameter of about three inches. They contained copper cylinders and iron strips isolated from each other by asphalt. Copper sulphate was found on the bottom of the vessels. By adding water an electrical current could be generated by these primitive batteries, sufficiently charged for gold- or silver-plating by galvanization. The most ancient of these batteries goes back to 250 B.C.; the most recent was made around A.D. 650. Galvanically gold-plated objects have also been excavated.

Galvani invented the electrical process named after him in 1791, and in 1800 Volta created the first battery of our culture, the Volta column. Fewer than two hundred years have therefore been available to us to explore the possible uses of electricity. The ancient magicians on the other hand had more than two thousand years. The possibility cannot be excluded that they discovered uses for it that are unknown to us today.

The secret of electricity seems to have been well guarded. Electricity is never mentioned directly in the alchemistic or magical scrolls. On the other hand there is a whole series of hidden allusions which point in this direction. There are references to lamps burning with a cold light, to apparatuses resembling the electrical instruments common in doctors' practices, to apparatuses for the reproduction of pictures, which remind one of electrical photography or xerography. The study of such ancient writings could be worthwhile for a modern technologist.

The dyeing of metals, the manufacture of red, blue, or black gold, of white gold, the creation of transparent metals—all these techniques are alluded to in the literature of alchemy. We no longer have reason to shrug off these allusions as old wives' tales. There may well have been electrochemical processes—ion displacement, global transference of ionized gas—of which we are still ignorant today. The ancients possessed inexhaustible patience; it is thoroughly conceivable that they treated a metal or an alloy for an entire century, through four generations, electrolytically or electrochemically, until the metal either changed its color or became transparent. Using our modern techniques, especially high-frequency alternating current, we may find a way to have these processes run their course in a few seconds. But the first step has to be to tackle the problem, and that is not being done. The Soviet Union is the only country in which science is making increasingly greater inroads into this area. Their research is raising a number of fresh problems. Near Tashkent for instance some remarkable finds have been made: clay vessels sealed with a kind of plastic. Their contents were limited to a large drop of mercury. The purpose of the vessels is not known. A description of them with illustrations was published in the Soviet periodical *The Modern Technologist.* If they were made of glass it could be assumed that they were apparatuses for the generation of static electricity or sources of light; Piccardi has demonstrated that low-frequency electromagnetic waves result when mercury is shaken in glass. They are of sufficient strength to make a neon light tube glow. But this result is not possible with a vessel made of clay. So what is the purpose of the vessels? We are in the position an intelligent man of the twelfth century would have found himself in had he been shown a transformer or a transistor.

WATER AND ITS SECRETS

Again and again in magical scrolls the wonderful properties of water from certain springs or of specially treated water are stressed.

Until recently this whole problem was considered to be just nonsense. In the meantime, however, it has been discovered that the water molecule has a malleable, semicrystalline structure. Transformations can take place under the influence of the forces surrounding a mineral or organic molecule. This factor explains why water forms hydrates that could not have been foreseen by the chemistry of classical antiquity, especially hydrates from natural gas. Natural or artificially generated magnetic fields can also effect the transformations, as was discovered by Piccardi. The great Florentine scientist discovered that certain colloidal reactions vary in speed according to the time of year. He drew the conclusion that the earth cuts across the lines of force of a magnetic field and that the chemical, physical, and biological properties of water are thus subject to seasonal variation. He proved in addition that water can be activated by electromagnetic waves of low frequency.

We know today that water is capable of changing its structure. It can work as a solvent, and on colloids it can have a stabilizing or disintegrating effect which normally it does not emanate. The conclusion must be that certain medications, poisons, and catalysts will vary in their effects according to the composition of the water in which they are dissolved, and indeed even according to the time of year when the substances are dissolved in the water! Research into this subject is still in its beginnings. It could be very considerably advanced if the descriptions of activated water to be found in large number in the literature of magic were heeded more.

HYPNOSIS AND SUGGESTION

Hypnosis was regarded for a long time as an occult practice. Today it has been so demystified that medical insurance even covers treatment by hypnosis in Great Britain.

But the literature of magic goes beyond magic, and contains many allusions to phenomena of positive or negative suggestion. A good magician has to be able to create optical illusions before a large audience of wide-awake spectators—for instance the Indian rope trick, or the trick with the plant that seems to grow out of the fakir's clay pot.

But according to the magical tradition it is equally possible to create negative hallucinations, which have the effect of preventing a person from seeing another person. This method of becoming invisible is said to be in use among thieves in India and Polynesia. Is it fair to deny without proof that there exist techniques of generating hysterical blindness or collective hallucinations? If such techniques do in fact exist, it would be interesting to investigate them scientifically. The phenomenon does not seem to have anything to do with hallucinatory drugs. Reliable witnesses have testified to the fact that the spectators were not under the influence of drugs. It seems that methods are used capable of influencing the appropriate nerve centers, so that the hallucinatory images or noises emanate from the hypnotized person himself. The person hypnotizes himself, as it were.

Photographs will not record hallucinations. Is this factor true also of a photographic cell or an electrostatic detector? This is not known. An article in the July 1959 issue of the English periodical *Fate* described experiments made by Mayne R. Coe, who claims to have succeeded in altering the electromagnetic field surrounding his body to such an extent that a measuring device reacted to it.

Is it possible to alter the field of force surrounding the human body in such a way that the nerve centers are influenced and hallucinations are generated? Can an electrostatic signal of this kind be modulated? Experimental studies on this subject do seem to be possible. The question is legitimate as to whether the power of certain historical figures such as Hitler was not bound up with a magic of this kind. In a seminar at the Sorbonne on the power of images Raymond Aron made the statement that the influence of politicians like Napoleon, Hitler, or Lenin could not be explained simply by the facts we know. Perhaps when a certain type of person has hallucinations he can generate hallucinations in others. Can an influence of this kind also be transmitted by radio and television? These questions are mind-boggling, surely meriting in the search for a reply a tiny fraction of the millions spent on motivational research. Can the ability to generate hallucinations be absorbed by inanimate objects and radiated out again? Is this the explanation, the rational kernel, of the countless legendary tales about talismans? Can a thing be so electrically charged that it can cause hallucinations in those close to it? We are not posing these questions as some kind of joke, but in order to awaken curiosity and stimulate research on the subject.

MAGIC AND SCENTED SUBSTANCES

Magic hints that an unfailing method of generating illusions and hallucinations or gaining power over a large crowd consists in the use of appropriate powders. Modern chemistry has analyzed and produced countless powders, and the literature on the subject is correspondingly voluminous. But the similarity between the structure of the molecules in certain powders like musk and that of deoxyribonucleic acid has to our knowledge never been pointed out. These approximations are obvious just by looking over the respective formulas. Like the molecules of nucleic acids, the powder molecules are of very complex structure, and can therefore be information-carriers. This aspect alone would justify serious study of the substances, whereby the research would have to be based not only on the science of information but also on the ancient magical texts, a great many of which refer to scented powders. A perfume capable of transmitting more information than the perfumes in use today, which becomes indispensable once one has acquired the habit of using it . . . Such an investigation would prove in addition that the magicians of antiquity knew much more about the psychological effects of perfumes than the best specialists of our own time.

AN ATTEMPT AT AN EXPLANATION

For us, building our arguments on facts rather than prejudices, there is no doubt at all that magic often attains results superior to those of our modern technology. For that reason we would like to try to explain this phenomenon rationally.

First we would like to make clear what is meant by the concept. Every person is free to believe that our entire world is only an illusion, a delusion of the senses. For the person who takes this view magic is no problem. One illusion is simply replaced by another. Our opinion however is that the world really exists and the means to exercise material influence upon this real world must *ipso facto* be technological in nature, through machines, chemical products, and so on. The human body is also a kind of machine, from which performances of a certain kind can be expected. In believing so, we agree with J.B.S. Haldane and Arthur C. Clarke. Assuming this position implies a decision. Either one denies systematically all phenomena that come under the rubric of magic, or one tries to explain them.

The facts we have provided—and they represent only a small selection—cannot be regarded simply as wild flights of the imagination. But if it is facts that are under discussion, some explanation has to be sought. We will do this in three ways.

FIRST HYPOTHESIS: CHANCE

It is conceivable that magic could be based on chance. The thesis would be that the magicians had been trying everything possible over a long period of time and had then stumbled on their discoveries by chance. They let themselves be guided solely by their imaginations and started from ideas or analogies that had no necessary connection at all with the results they were striving for. This explanation is favored by Gaston Bachelard. He is of the opinion that "the creation of fire by the rubbing of a stick through a hole bored in a piece of wood was inspired by the similarity of this movement with that of the life- and strength-giving male sex organ inside the organ of the female." But this simplifying thesis seems to be applicable only to extremely rudimentary techniques. If the aim is to explain the generation of a plant alkaloid by complicated chemical processes, or the manufacture of aluminum bronze, or the thousands of other apparatuses and products one finds described in magical writings, the hypothesis of chance will not go very far. It would be just as valid to claim that the inventors of the airplane did not know what they were doing, or were simply trying to imitate the sparrows.

SECOND HYPOTHESIS: A KNOWLEDGE
HIGHER THAN SCIENCE

This second attempted explanation will necessarily annoy all scientists, since it claims nothing less than that magic draws from sources superior to those of the experimental method, that magicians in a trance can learn everything that scientists have to labor over in a slow endeavor to extract from nature. G.N.M. Tyrrell, the great English parapsychologist, writes, "The scientific periodical with the largest circulation in the world, *Nature,* has as its motto: 'The scientific mind turns to the solid source of nature.' ''

It is almost as though nature were looked upon as a rival. But it is of course understandable that a scientist who has been working in pharmaceutical chemistry for twenty-five years despairs when told that a Chinese pharmacist and mystic has attained better results through ''revelation.''

We do believe that there is such a thing as a spiritual reality and that contact with this reality can lead to strange phenomena about which hardly anything is yet known, for instance to mystical ecstasy. But does this spiritual reality deliver the comprehensive description of a Reverbier oven, a refraction chamber, and a regenerator? The Chinese needed such ovens to manufacture their aluminum. In our opinion magic is based more on technology than on spiritual realities, even if these do exist.

THIRD HYPOTHESIS: ANCIENT KNOWLEDGE

It is probably necessary to admit that the magicians have always had technological knowledge at their disposal. The data in their possession was perhaps distorted and fragmentary; nevertheless it was technological information. Where did it come from? Only one source would come into question: lost cultures that had attained a higher level of technological advance than we have, and of which a few traces have been preserved in the rites and alchemistic recipes.

This hypothesis will bring a cry of protest from all archaeologists. They will say: But up to now not a trace has been found of such cultures! Then what about the Chinese aluminum bronze with precision mechanism found on the island of Antikytheros, what about the iron column at Delhi that is incorrosible, and what about many other finds at present classified under ''miscellaneous?'' The Baghdad batteries were displayed at museums for a long time as ''cult objects.'' Sir David Brewster found optical lenses in a tomb in Persia much better than anything that could be manufactured in his day. The list of such examples could be continued indefinitely. The day will perhaps come when it is admitted that cultures too are ephemeral and objects that cannot be classified were once scientific instruments, long-distance communications apparatuses, fragments of a technological plant or a technological instrument. On that day we will without doubt recognize the lost culture, reflected still in magic as in a dark glass, as part of a mighty cycle.

—Jacques Bergier

How We Will Live in 1984

Which year is closer: 1900 or 2000? Ask the people on the streets; most of them will say: 2000!

HOW I SEE OUR FUTURE

The future is in the works; its outlines are already recognizable, even if some of its details are still beyond our ken. Many products and installations that twenty years ago did not even have a name play a part in our life today. The broad contours of the future are already visible. Our prognosis will be accurate short of some worldwide catastrophe such as a nuclear war.

On the basis of present-day knowledge it is possible to construct a model for the immediate future, up to about the year 1984. It is possible to say already that 1984 will not be as George Orwell described it in his famous novel. He predicted for this era a merciless dictatorship in a dehumanized world. It is certain that this will not happen because the world as it is being prepared in the laboratories looks quite different.

The immediate future will be an age of electricity. The possible forms of energy have been well known for a long time, but most countries in the world have hardly benefitted from them. There are two reasons for this: 1) we are still not able to conserve electricity or produce it in light, small plants; and 2) electricity is manufactured by the conversion of the energy contained in natural fuels (coal, crude oil). In twenty years we will be using atomic and solar energy for this purpose.

The language of the near future should include these expressions: fuel element, solar battery, small generator, cadmium-nickel accumulator.

These expressions will have tremendous significance for our everyday life, for the electromobile will be the vehicle of tomorrow. It will use gasoline as fuel, but in a new and economical way. The energy released by the fuel will be converted directly into electricity through contact with oxygen from the air. The vehicle will therefore need less fuel. Its ride will be quiet and smooth. Its braking distance will be short, because it will brake by reversal of the electrical current in the wheels. The brakes will be mounted directly onto the street as completely flat strips in front of the vehicle.

The entire world will be affected by this changeover to the electromobile, first of all commercially, because the electromobile will rescue an industry already struggling with a saturated market. The traffic problem in cities will be solved by the new vehicle. The probability is that private cars will no longer be permitted; in their place there will be small cars for hire, all standardized and capable of being activated for a certain time by the insertion of a coin. Once the occupant has arrived at his destination he simply leaves the car where it is.

Such vehicles will be intended only for city use. For driving outside big cities, and especially on highways, the electromobile offers definite advantages. Equipment can be built in to prevent accidents and to program journeys. To prevent accidents a kind of radar installation will be built in and powered by the engine current. Programmed driving in 1984 will mean that the driver inserts a punch card into the vehicle's electronic computer. If he is in New York and wants to go to Boston, the card is punched accordingly and the vehicle makes the journey by the shortest route without the driver needing to concern himself further. Vehicles of this kind have already been tested in the United States on short, special roads. A driver's license would no longer be necessary.

Apart from the electromobile there will be thousands of appliances similar to those of today: vacuum cleaners, electric drills, toasters, irons, and so on. But they will be enormously different in one respect. They will no longer need to be plugged in to the electric current, but will be driven instead by an independent source of energy. The first drills with accumulator drive were manufactured in 1963. In twenty years all electrical appliances will be independent of the plug. This "liberation" of electricity will have consequences for everyday life hard to imagine today. The new appliances will make their own electricity out of fuel by means of small converters or fuel elements, or contain a built-in chargeable cadmium-nickel accumulator. It is possible that even in solar batteries accumulators will convert the solar energy into electricity. Domestic chores will be made considerably easier by these innovations. The age of electricity will then really have properly begun. Air pollution will gradually disappear with the gradual elimination of the combustion engine. Housing developments will be built with every comfort and convenience—refrigerators, air-conditioning, television sets—and it will be possible to locate them far from all power plants and at any selected place on earth. All that will be needed to supply electric power for the whole settlement will be a few barrels of fuel and a converter.

In underdeveloped countries life will be completely transformed by electricity. It will be possible to produce artificial manure and build up industries. Here the key words are nuclear reactor and magneto-hydrodynamic generator. The nuclear reactor creates heat by uranium fission and the magneto-hydrodynamic generator converts this heat directly into electricity. The plants would, however, be huge, economical only with high consumption. They will soon be seen everywhere in the world, but especially in industrially backward countries. In such countries they will be the most vital sources of energy and will provide a new impetus to life. In 1984 the measure of the stage of development of a country looked upon today as underdeveloped will be the number of its energy generators. The export of such generators will be the most important form of industrial expansion for industrial nations, and the competition in this field the most active form of the Cold War.

THE BATTLE OF THE WATERS WILL BE WON

In twenty years the Cold War will be on in another area, in the battle for water. Today the world is already suffering from a shortage of drinking water. In 1984 this crisis will be far more acute. To make up for this shortage it will be necessary to convert seawater into drinking water, using electricity. Let us therefore add another word to our vocabulary of the future: electromembrane. An electromembrane is an electrically charged papyrus filter that lets through water but retains the salts dissolved in it. When seawater is used it is possible to extract iodine, magnesium, gold, and other useful substances from the residue in the membrane. Giant power plants with nuclear reactors and magneto-hydrodynamic generators to manufacture electricity will pump whole rivers of drinking water from the sea. New cities will rise on the banks of these rivers; deserts will bloom with flowers. These artificial sources of drinking water will bear the flag of the country that erected them and will represent its technology in the Third World. Sources of drinking water will take the place of military conquest as the witness to the might and state of technological progress of the country that created them.

In 1964 the Soviets began the construction of a giant installation for the desalination of the Caspian Sea at Chevchenko. It is designed to supply 25 million gallons of drinking water per day, and be fueled by what is allegedly the largest nuclear reactor in the world, the gigantic BR-250. The Americans have already accepted the challenge and are planning still larger plants in Israel, Egypt, Kuwait, the Mexican deserts, and North Africa. These desalination plants will be as familiar a sight to the people of 1984 as the big steel works and power plants of our own time are to us. Their mighty, smokeless chimneys (chimneys are needed to enable the cooling gases from the reactors to escape) will be a reminder that the reserves of our planet are not unlimited and that the dreadful problems of overpopulation remain threateningly on the horizon. For even by 1984 the population explosion will not have been brought to a standstill.

HOW DOES ONE AVOID BEING A NUMBER?

The main problem will be how to preserve the balance between the individual and society, how to make sure that the individual is not reduced to a mere number.

The man of 1984 will start out by being a ten-digit number. He will carry this number around with him all his life. It will be imprinted in magnetic dye on an identification card, enabling him by producing it to cash a check at any bank anywhere in the world. The number will also permit him to be reached by telephone at any time and any place, provided he keeps his nearest telephone exchange informed of changes of address. The number will be so digited as to indicate his blood group, his medical history, and his citizenship. In the case of a man suspected of a crime, it will suffice to supply Interpol with his number in order to close to him all means of transportation. Giant electronic computers will store data on every number and will provide in seconds information on a man's profession, standard of living, and so on. World health authorities and other international organizations will have access to this information, these "magnetic files." The number will make every individual of 1984 a world citizen.

But he will be more than just a number. He will be able to defend himself against society, which may be fatherly toward him but nevertheless too inquisitive and powerful. One word in particular will be heard constantly: ombudsman. The ombudsman is the most revolutionary social invention of the twentieth century, even more revolutionary than Communism. The concept of the ombudsman originated in the Scandinavian countries, where the ombudsman is an official whose job it is to defend the individual against the government. Elected by a small group of citizens, he cannot be displaced and is unbribable. Anyone who feels he has been discriminated against by society, by overtaxation, willful injustice, rejection, refusal of a passport, or whatever, has the ombudsman to turn to. The ombudsman takes on his case without charge and represents his rights vis-à-vis society and before the law.

In the Scandinavian countries there is a lot of discussion about how many ombudsmen are necessary. One ombudsman for every six thousand citizens is the proposed ratio. The Liberal Party in England has as part of its program the introduction of the ombudsman to Great Britain. In 1964 the Soviets announced their interest in the arrangement. In 1984 all people who do not want to be simply a number but also a name will be able to turn to their ombudsman. This innovation will provide a counterbalance in our overpossessive society.

But this arrangement will not solve all the ills of society. If, as some of the best minds believe, 1984 will bring world government, who will guard the guardians? Will it be within the capabilities of the ombudsmen, respected local administrative officials, to resist such an organism, which will be mightier than all dictatorships of earlier times, which will control the planet, have gigantic electronic brains at their disposal, know all there is to know about the techniques of psychological and psychochemical control? These are the questions the man of 1984 will put to himself when he looks at the unreadable punch card that serves him simultaneously as passport, checkbook, and health-control card. The future members of a world government, organizers and specialists, will pose these questions too. And one concept in particular will turn up in their discussions: the Stine curve.

ARE WE BECOMING IMMORTAL?

From 1950 to 1960 Harry Stine, rocket specialist and science-fiction author, set himself the task of calculating the curves which, as a function of time, reproduce the velocity of vehicles, energy production, and the density of traffic and communications networks. His aim was the same as that of André de Cayeux and Francois Meyer in France: to chart the acceleration of history. In this way he was able to predict the sputniks and a majority of the great advances in technology. He also set up other curves, in particular the curve relating to the duration of life. It was this curve that showed an astounding and yet frightening fact: a child born in the year 2000 has good prospects of not dying at all—ever. The curve of life expectancy climbs steeply in the year 2000 and tends toward infinity.

In 1984 this development will already have moved into the more immediate future. The deciphering of the genetic code and discoveries in the realm of the chemistry of life are bringing the moment near when immortality will become a reality—at least for some people. For the scientists of 1984 will realize clearly that if the life of a child born in the year 2000 is to be prolonged for several centuries or even a millennium—the chosen person would be preserved physically in the condition of a fifty-year-old—the efforts of an army of first-rate biologists and the expenditure of vast sums of money will be required.

Who will choose the children for such favored treatment? This question is particularly urgent because the number will have to be kept strictly limited, in the twenty-first century perhaps to a dozen. Will it be the world government that has this right? Who will then be in a position to prevent the members from choosing their own children for the gift of immortality? Public opinion? That can easily be influenced. The ombudsmen? They are entrusted only with local problems. Already the shadow of immortality is beginning to fall across mankind with all the conflicts that it can generate.

And yet there will be immortality someday. It will take several centuries to assimilate all the knowledge that is won day by day. It will also be many centuries before man reaches the stars beyond our solar system in flying torches, those spaceships driven by light that are now being developed. The immortals are necessary, but how can they be chosen from among mortals? That will be the big question of 1984, which will come up again and again in intellectual discussions.

PROBLEMS THAT HAVE SOLVED THEMSELVES

And yet mankind of 1984 will not be disturbed. It will have witnessed too often how problems have solved themselves. The struggle between communism and capitalism will be over. Both forms of society will exist alongside each other, and their conflict will be forgotten as were the religious wars of yesteryear. In 1984 a registered member of the Communist Party will be able to walk the streets of New York freely, and the propagandist of aggressive neocapitalism will remain unharmed in Moscow. All a man will need will be his world number and his magnetic card. As long as the magnetic card shows that his account is covered, he will be able to get dollars in New York and rubles in Moscow.

The problem of leisure time will also be solved, by private initiative. For many years people who despised youth, freedom, and beauty were inclined to ram the dictum down our throats that man cannot tolerate an age of leisure, that the thirty-hour week is a catastrophe, and that our youth will go mad. The same statements were made in the nineteenth century about the fifty-two-hour week. In 1984 the thirty-hour week of 1972 will be followed by the twenty-four-hour week. It will not lead to catastrophe. The truth is rather that the liberation of energies stored during leisure time and vacations will lead to one of the greatest intellectual revolutions in the history of mankind.

THE LANGUAGE OF SCIENCE FOR EVERYMAN

Another key word of 1984 will be Lansi.

As early as 1940 it was clear that none of the languages spoken and written on earth was really suitable for teaching science. Benjamin Lee Whorf has demonstrated clearly that the Eastern languages like Russian and Chinese do not correspond to the real universe, the universe of relativity and quanta. For that reason scientific culture has become accessible to everyone only since the invention of Lansi, the *langage scientifique,* or scientific language.

The inventors of this language have taken into account and combined the research of Whorf, the investigations of Gilbert Cohen-Séat on purely rational languages like Logalan, research on languages of communication between man and machine (Cobo, Algol), and Gérard Cordonnier's ideas about a metalanguage. Lansi, invented in the seventies, is the scientific language corresponding to the world's needs. It has neither nouns nor verbs. It describes events in the space-time system and indicates their probability. Fifteen years at most are necessary to master Lansi, and then the entire corpus of scientific literature can be read.

A popular scientific work written in Lansi stays in the memory of its own accord, and is immediately taken in and understood. The old teaching methods are comparable to human food before the discovery of fire, that is to say, hard to digest. On the intellectual level Lansi is the equivalent of food prepared with the help of heat. Science translated into Lansi can be digested immediately. Radiochemical printing methods will permit cheap reproduction and free distribution of scientific works to billions of people. The only comparable revolutionary invention was the invention of writing.

Naturally Lansi presents a few problems. The most difficult problem concerns intellectually retarded people. Whoever has the desire to make Lansi and the treasures of science accessible to himself must have an intelligence quotient of at least 80 (the average is 100). Unfortunately, the number of people with an intelligence quotient of below 80 is far greater than has been assumed, especially in highly industrialized countries. These people, cut off from progress, represent a minority exposed to a very undesirable fate. A minority that would like to escape from that fate. A minority that has been a victim of charlatans all too often.

In 1984 no week will go by without warnings from the World Health Organization about pills supposed to increase intelligence but which in fact are useless and likely to cause cancer. New pseudoreligious cults and pseudohypnotic methods will make promises of raising I.Q.s to make the acquisition of Lansi possible for everybody. There will be advertisements offering the discreet forwarding of intelligence-improvement courses. And it will all be nothing but a swindle. In a few isolated cases it has been possible to increase intelligence through the inhalation of positive ions (the method was developed during the sixties by Dr. Dussert de Bergerac), but the method can be successfully applied only under very special circumstances. It seems mankind is split into two parts. The aim is to have all men born equal, but unfortunately that aim cannot be realized for the moment.

NEW SCIENCES

Will there come a point of saturation? Will the interest in science be just a passing fad? No one can say yet. It seems probable that the interest of men will turn more and more inward, toward the secrets of human personality. The wonders of the outside world, the fantastic phenomena of reality, seem to move the masses far less.

The discovery of the lost city of Atlantis, the traces of a form of primitive life found in caverns on the moon, the breathtaking riches in the dead cities of Mars, all that has inspired only the young. On the other hand there is a growing general interest in telepathy, the collective subconscious, mystical ecstasy, and so on. Many distinguished scientists are most willing to take part in controlled parapsychological experiments. Since by 1984 telepathic communication between the earth and the moon will have been established, nobody will still doubt the reality of parapsychology. The great name will be C. G. Jung.

THE SCIENCE OF DESTINY

More and more scientists will be seeking to prove the theory of synchronization postulated by C.G. Jung and the Nobel Prize winner

Pauli. This theory, which gives the ancient concept of fate a scientific underpinning through the idea that every man can be the master of the destiny determined for him through genetic and social factors, will form the axis of completely new sciences combining cosmology, psychology, and mathematics. Young people will dream of becoming cosmic observers or destinologists. These professions will certainly be very difficult, but they will form the hub, the most significant orientation of science.

Nuclear physics will have created a new profession, that of the nuclear technologist, who like everyone else will work a twenty-four-hour week. Research in mathematics will also become routine, a good, solid profession, but no longer one capable of generating excitement. The new sciences, which will combine physics and psychology, will attract the best minds.

The man and woman on the street will feel strongly affected by discoveries like synchronization and the analysis of fate, and these discoveries will give rise to new religions.

A NEW RELIGIOUS WAR

Subud, founded in the fifties by the Indonesian Pak Subud, will have spread over the entire world. By 1984 Subud will have more supporters in Indonesia than Islam. In Communist countries, Subud will have gained more ground in China and Soviet Central Asia than anywhere else. In Africa it will be the predominant religion.

In the ancient Islamic world the Bahai religion will have increased in strength despite all efforts at suppression, and will have conquered practically the entire Mediterranean area; at the same time this religion will have greatly improved its following in Great Britain and the United States.

In North America, Scandinavia, and, remarkably enough, Italy, the cult of the Giants of the Galaxies, at first held to be some sort of mental aberration to do with flying saucers, will have experienced an unforeseen rise in popularity and will have between 5 and 6 million supporters. The doctrines of this cult will maintain that representatives from the Federation of Galaxies, the same intelligences that transmitted the signals picked up by radiotelescopes, will pay visits to the earth. Anthropologists will compare this new religion with the Polynesian cargo cult. Satirists will make fun of it. Yet in 1984 about 6 million people will believe in the imminent arrival of the Giants of the Galaxies in their interstellar spaceships, and will persist in that belief despite all the arguments of scientists that interstellar space can be overcome only with great difficulty by short-lived beings like men. In India new religions based on the experiences of racial consciousness that revive the old cultish beliefs in reincarnation will spread to the disadvantage of the more ancient beliefs.

Ecumenical congresses will try to unite the traditional religions in order to survive the struggle against the new religions. Historians, psychologists, and sociologists will occupy themselves with the study of the new religions, their origins, and the reasons for their power. Mystics will deny their genuineness and recognize only the classical revelations: Moses, Jesus, and Mohammed. By 1984 rationalists will have disappeared completely. The few left will see in the spread of new religions a sign of human degeneration.

DRUGS, TIME, AND SPACE

From a certain calorie intake onward—around three thousand calories daily—along with a certain leisure time, say two full days per week, there arises a certain need for the supernatural, the miraculous, for what Jung called the "vitamins of the soul." Science will be able to satisfy it just as little as science fiction or the traditional religions. Will the new religions provide satisfaction? The question is urgent.

Some men were convinced, following the publication of Aldous Huxley's brilliant books *Heaven and Hell* and *The Doors of Perception,* that there were drugs capable of enriching life in such a way that the unknown guest, that which can be called soul, consciousness, or psyche, contained the vitamins he needed.

By 1984, it will be clear that psilocybin and mescaline are far more dangerous and addictive than was earlier assumed. Hundreds of other synthetic drugs will have been manufactured, none of them harmless. For that reason their use will have been forbidden by law; they will be taken only under the supervision of a doctor.

And yet it cannot be denied that these drugs seem to have unusual properties—some of them stimulating parapsychological capacities. At least one hundred patients—all of them under the influence of LSD—will have experienced the Chinese earthquake of 1978 three years earlier in a dream. Other experiments of this kind will have demonstrated that taking certain drugs induces a trancelike vision of the past, the future, and sometimes perhaps other worlds. That will be one of the most exciting adventures of the year 1984. Volunteers will be called for to test new drugs just as in 1964 volunteers were needed for the space program. The fate of many of these volunteers will be death, of others, madness. The survivors, however, will tell tales of having experienced documentable scenes from the past or visions of the future destined to be fulfilled, or they will describe other worlds that exist perhaps elsewhere in the universe. These worlds will turn up in the dreams of volunteers who have nothing to do with each other. Probably every world corresponds to a different drug. At this "inner frontier" man awaits the great discoveries which will shake the world of 1984.

MAN IS NO LONGER DISSATISFIED

In what directions will men's hopes go in 1984? Between 1980 and 1984 the world television network and the major periodicals will carry out a worldwide referendum, during which 700 million people (including a roughly equal number of men and women) will be asked that question. Ninety per cent will express the hope of receiving some proof of immortality or reincarnation. All will agree that "something as glorious as the human person" could not simply disappear like a hole in a piece of paper when the paper burns. But although this hope will not have been realized through parapsychological discoveries nor through any of the experiments with drugs, it will remain alive and widespread. This factor will perhaps be explained through the spread of the new religions, since the old religions were never able to prove immortality.

Two possibilities for physical immortality will be real in 1984: immortality for a small number of children who receive a special treatment, and immortality through hibernation for those who are daring enough to be put into a hundred-year sleep in liquid helium. But neither of these alternatives is really satisfying, and the man of 1984 will still harbor hopes that the new science will succeed where the old sciences and the old religions failed: in supplying proof that there is another life.

—Jacques Bergier

War Games with Electronic Computers

The general desirous of winning a battle makes many calculations in his temple beforehand.
—Sun Tsu (Chinese general), 500 B.C.

A MAD WORLD

When the United States entered the First World War in 1917, its government was faced with difficult problems. A preliminary estimate had put the figure of draftable Americans at 500,000. Now the decision had to be made when to mobilize them. To draft them too soon would be pointless, yet to call them up too late could have catastrophic consequences. The problem was put to several statisticians and mathematicians, whose solutions were contradictory. In the end Colonel Leonard P. Ayres, an Army statistics expert, was entrusted with the task. Ayres submitted a report to the President in which he stated that after precise mathematical calculations he had come to the conclusion that the most favorable time to mobilize would be the month of September 1917. And indeed, everything went well. Nobody asked Colonel Ayres how he had arrived at his decision, and he made his method known only on May 4, 1940, before a class of officer cadets, when the Second World War was heading for the United States.

Colonel Ayres's method had consisted of working out the date when the recruitment centers would be able to supply every new recruit with a pair of uniform trousers; he regarded this particular item of military apparel as the minimum for the setting up of an army. The various calculations made available to him he had simply ignored.

Colonel Ayres's trousers are generally considered to be the first example of what is now called operations research, which is to say the application of sophisticated analytical methods to phenomena too complicated to be analyzed solely through mathematics. Operations research and its more advanced version, generally called systems analysis, have gained astounding prestige in the United States. Over recent years laboratories have been created in which men and machines fight imaginary battles, with the aim not of winning a real war but rather of preventing war. These laboratories are controlled by the Rand Corporation (Rand = Research and Development), the most unusual private organization on our planet. Until recently, military secrecy sealed Rand off virtually hermetically from the outside world. The tip of the veil of secrecy was lifted in the book *Analysis for Military Decision,* edited by Edward S. Quade. The authors of the contributions are too numerous to be named here, but all are members of the Rand Corporation. The book is not the official voice either of the Rand Corporation or of the American Air Force, which is advised by Rand. With this reservation, the book is an extraordinarily fine source of information, which I have drawn on extensively in preparing this essay.

MARTIANS INVADE THE EARTH

As will be seen, neither imagination nor humor are lacking in the Rand Corporation book. Yet its theme is a significant one, and the continued existence of mankind could depend on many of the considerations dealt with in the work. The aim of the investigations is to prevent the chance outbreak of accidental war, and to prevent the destruction of the United States and subsequently the whole world. The specialists feed into the computer not only precise data based on known fact, but also a whole series of data representing the unknown, chance. This mass of information, contained on as many as several thousand punch cards for a single programming, is called "Monte Carlo."

One of the investigations concerns a project which according to the authors consists of a plan to invade the earth with flying saucers manufactured on Mars. This improbable problem is typical of the work carried on in these laboratories. First the mathematicians graph the curve of the surmised production of flying saucers, basing their calculations on costs and available work force. The flying saucers are presumed to be brought by ship along the Mars canals to the storage depots, which means there is a problem of logistics to be considered. The flight curves of the flying saucers in the various gravitational fields of the earth have to be worked out, and the gravitational fields of Mars and of the satellites of both Mars and the earth must be taken into consideration. At this stage in the calculations the flying saucer can be represented by a dot.

Once the flying saucer has entered the earth's atmosphere, however, the dot becomes insufficient as a symbol for the spaceship, and has to be replaced by an aerodynamic model. As soon as the flying saucer has been picked up by radar in the earth's atmosphere and airplanes have gone up to head it off, the model must be subjected to constant alterations and improvements. This problem seems to have been solved in masterly fashion by the Martian colleagues of the men from Rand, since to date not one single flying saucer from Mars has been shot down or forced to land. In these laboratories not only man-made wars are studied but also the possibility of wars unleashed by unknown enemies.

DISMANTLE THE PLANES TO KEEP THEM SAFE

It is of course strictly forbidden to publish reports on the imaginary wars waged by the technologists of Rand in the recent past. The world moves too fast for that. Until a short time ago the airplane was the most important weapon. Documents released by the Rand Corporation describe a few imaginary wars waged in 1956. Let it be said immediately that the majority of these wars were lost. Most of the American air bases were situated too close to Soviet air bases for attack warnings to be provided early enough. The illustrations and descriptions document this point amply. The problem had to be thought through again and redefined in terms of the defeats experienced. The problem was to make the American bombers as invulnerable as possible while keeping their availability unrestricted. Some of the solutions arrived at by mathematical methods are reminiscent in their black humor of certain unforgettable scenes from the film *Doctor Strangelove*. With the support of electronic computers one mathematician suggested that in order to protect the aircraft of the Strategic Air Command most effectively from Soviet surprise attacks the best plan was to take the planes apart and bury them somewhere in the Antarctic. Unfortunately they would no longer have been in a position to inflict any damage on the enemy.

Another means to protect the American bombers was to keep them permanently in the air, with airborne refueling from KB-36s. But to put this plan into operation more than 1700 KB-36s would have been necessary, far more than the Americans had at their disposal. All the same, this proposal was partially adopted, as is well known today. A certain number of U.S. bombers carrying atom bombs are always airborne. The same procedure is followed by the Soviets.

It took an IBM-704 about six hours of uninterrupted calculations to work out all the possibilities of a sixty-hour air war involving the air forces of the United States, the Soviet Union, and the allies of both sides. The electronic computer is fed with all the possible starting positions of both sides. Especially important is data concerning the strength of the air forces (bombers, refueling planes, transport planes, fighters), airfields, defensive installations (radar, missiles, fighter airfields). A series of contingency plans is then punched in for each side. These plans resemble strategic tables. They take account of the strength of the enemy forces possibly available in various locations, and cover various possible plans of action. Once all factual data has been fed in, the machine can begin with the actual war, which then takes its course without interruption. Approximately 150,000 punch cards are needed for such a sixty-hour war.

FALSE INTUITIONS ARE EXPENSIVE

In 1956 the Rand Corporation succeeded, after a number of computer operations, in winning an imaginary war against the Soviet Union. The victory was made possible by the positioning of several air bases on foreign soil. At any given moment only some of these bases were actually occupied, and the American bombers were transferred frequently and quickly from one base to another, so that the Soviets were able to destroy only a part of the bomber force.

Another very unusual imaginary war was based on the idea of luring the Soviets into a trap by making them believe the Strategic Air Command was vulnerable. The Russians could perhaps be enticed into concentrating all their air forces onto the bases of the Strategic Air Command in the United States. The Soviet planes would then be destroyed by flak and fighters, making the Americans the undisputed lords of the earth. But a thorough analysis of the plan revealed a grave weakness: since the Russians are only human and might make mistakes like anyone else, it was conceivable that during their massive attacks they would miss the air bases and the camouflaged dummies laid out all around them, and instead bomb cities like Washington, New York, and Los Angeles. The Soviets would then have needed only to continue the war until the final victory, according to mathematical logistics, without fearing American retaliation. In this imaginary war billions of dollars would have been invested in the effort to defeat the Russians, only to discover that it was the United States that was doomed.

A FUTURE POSSIBILITY: BASES ON THE MOON

The Rand Corporation concerns itself not only with the present but also with the future. E.W. Paxson has investigated the problems that the establishment of a base on the moon would raise. Like most Rand documents, this one displays remarkable black humor. There is for instance the following definition of a man, borrowed from the Hungarian-born American expert on aerodynamics, von Karman: "Man is an extraordinarily efficient mechanical brain manufactured by workers without any special skills but produced cheaply and with enthusiasm."

Rand envisions a base on the moon as a permanently manned military support garrison on the trabant of the earth. Calculations have shown that the erection of such a base will be a practical possibility when American industry has developed a nuclear—electrical—engine capable of producing a thrust of 1000 kilowatts per kilogram of weight. We are still a long way from that point; about ten tons are needed for every megawatt of thrust. But the technological progress graph suggests that man will be able to manufacture an engine of this type in the not-too-distant future. From that moment on it will be possible to calculate all that is necessary for the establishment of a base on the moon, as Rand is already doing. One of the first tasks of such a base will be to produce nuclear fuel elements on the moon itself, for use in the propulsion of rockets. In this case it would be possible to reduce very considerably (by about 80 per cent) the weight of the fuel load necessary for a journey to the moon and back. The journey will not actually be from the earth to the moon but between space stations, one orbiting the earth, the other orbiting the moon. This is not science fiction. Everything has already been worked out and planned down to the last detail, with tables and illustrations, in the manner of planning a new bus station.

Travel between a space station orbiting the earth and the earth's surface, or between the moon and a moon satellite, will be accomplished in traditional rocket ships fired by chemical fuels. On the other hand, travel from the earth to a moon satellite will be fueled by atomic energy. The traveler will receive a sort of diagram like the blueprint of a factory, with the difference that our diagram will provide complete details of the colonization of the moon, the establishment of bases, hydroponic hothouses (hydroponics is the science of plant cultivation without soil), rabbit farms in which the animals are fed on algae and mushrooms grown on the spot, fuel factories, and finally, observation stations and military bases directed against the earth—all developments planned to take place in the next twenty-five years or so.

From the moon the earth could be observed through instruments equipped with lenses having a diameter of only ten meters. Rockets carrying nuclear warheads could be launched from the moon to any point on the earth. These developments are all being discussed soberly from strictly mathematical, almost bookkeeping perspectives. There is no concern for the possible impact of a lunar base on politics or psychology, and no consideration is given to what might happen if mankind were forced to live under a permanent threat of attack from the moon.

THREE DOCUMENTS TOWARD THE PREVENTION OF THE IRREVOCABLE

The Rand report mentions secondary literature, although in a brief summary form. Especially striking is an article of the "Robinson Crusoe" type. In it the possibility of some catastrophe cutting off all communication between the earth and the lunar station is discussed. In such an event the inhabitants of the base would have to try to survive for a certain time on their own.

Does the research of the Rand Corporation permit a prediction about what will happen in the real world? This question is not easy to answer. It is certain that the work of the organization is followed very carefully by the American General Staff, and is extensively consulted during the formulation of important documents pertaining to the General Staff. Documents under constant process of revision are:

1. The *Joint Strategic Capability Plan,* which analyzes the future one year at a time. Its contents are concerned mainly with purely military matters.

2. The *Joint Strategic Operating Plan,* which concerns itself with the development of new weapons, their mass production and their production costs, and extends its perspectives over the next ten years.

3. The *Joint Long-Range Strategic Study,* which considers the next fourteen years and examines mainly the political aspects.

What international alliances will be formed? What major international crises will occur? In what way will the United States have to intervene? With what means? How far will they have to go? The final escalation is a general thermonuclear war on the earth, the moon, and in interplanetary space. Are these plans often changed? Nobody of course knows the answer to this question with any certainty, and it is therefore impossible to say whether the Rand Corporation predictions about the future are accurate. The opinion of Rand specialists is that production costs can increase tenfold over the best estimates, and an assessed delay can vary up to five years. The electronic computers cannot err in their calculations, but the men responsible for the input could have asked the wrong questions or answered correct questions wrongly. In this field, thought to be so factually strict and sober, intuition plays a big part.

The favorite example at Rand is the problem of the commercial traveler. Suppose a traveler starting out from Washington has to visit the capitals of all the states in the union, then return to Washington to present his report. The problem is: What would be the shortest route? A first analysis through the electronic computer shows that there are 10^{61} possible solutions. A plan of operation shows that even with the best of computing equipment, solving of the problem would take so long that in the meantime the sun would have burned itself out and the earth frozen over.

After this not very encouraging result, a few Rand engineers set out to solve the problem from a quite different angle. They took a map, needles, and a roll of wool. Purely intuitively–5theyfound the shortest route in quarter of an hour. The ideal prediction of the future would consist of first developing an intuitive solution, testing this solution with the help of computers, then making the prediction.

But intuition can be misleading too. A typical example: Suppose all the armed forces of the United States, together with intercontinental ballistic missiles, bombers carrying atomic bombs, nuclear submarines, air defenses, death rays, and so on, were set up and on alert for the emergency defense of the country. A year goes by. The expected attack does not take place. In the meantime the American munitions industry produces other defense weapons, new firearms, rockets, radar installations, laser guns, and so on. Where should they be set up? The intuitive answer to this question is that the new weapons should be used to defend targets that up to now had remained defenseless for lack of appropriate munitions. This consideration may seem to make sense, but it is wrong. When a careful accounting is made of the facts, the conclusion is arrived at that the strengthening of the American defenses leads to a proportionate diminution of enemy power. The foe will thus have to concentrate on the most important targets, which must therefore be better defended even if they are already enjoying the best defense available at this time. That is not immediately obvious, but the calculations always come up with the same result. The original intuitive choice was wrong, but at least it turned the calculations in the right direction, even if the result was quite different than anticipated.

WHAT SORT OF PEOPLE ARE THEY?

In spite of a few scattered pieces of information invariably denied right away, the men of the Rand Corporation remain for the most part anonymous. It is not known how individuals are selected for entry into the Holy Shrine in Santa Monica, California. The Federal Bureau of Investigation investigates the background of all candidates back to nine months before they were born. The reason for this is that illegitimate birth could be used by foreign agents for blackmailing purposes. A Ph.D. in the natural sciences is required, as are good accounting skills; bookkeeping plays a large part in the research of the Rand Corporation. In addition the candidate must be a first-class mathematician. A few names are known: Edward S. Quade, J. Hitch, R.D. Specht, R.N. McKean, Malcolm W. Hoag, Albert Wohlsetter, R. Schamberg, T.C. Schelling, M.G. Weiner, W.H. Meckling, Paul Armer, E.W. Paxson. But there is no documentation to be found anywhere that provides information about the exact functions of these men; there is no material anywhere about the structure of the organization.

Just as little is known about whether the employees of Rand are obliged to submit to a psychological examination at the outset of their employment or at regular intervals while they are on the job. Such an investigation would seem to be advisable in view of the antics of a former employee of Rand, Hermann Kahn, who has now opened his own analytical practice. Hermann Kahn is the prototype of the Dr. Strangelove of the film. He invented the Doomsday machine, then published the plans of the machine. His investigations were carried out at the expense of the American government, which invested $73 million in them.

The Doomsday machine is a super-cobalt bomb, of which the fallout would be enough to destroy all life on earth. The bomb is connected to a computer that detonates it when a certain number of nuclear explosions have scourged the earth to a preprogrammed degree. With a humor worthy of Eichmann, Hermann Kahn maintains that that would be a deterrent to would-be aggressors. One comforting fact is that Rand itself distrusts machines invented and laboratory experiments carried out too quickly. The following memorable sentence is in one of the reports of the corporation: "All good ideas are born in the laboratory, are developed in the laboratory, and die in the laboratory, and for the most part the whole process lasts no longer than twenty minutes."

All the publications of the Rand Corporation stress the human aspect, the necessity for the greatest care, the practical aspect. Rand places emphasis upon bookkeeping knowledge and takes careful

account of the dollar value of a project in order not to fall victim to
superficial extravagances.

The influential American periodical *Space Aeronautics* raised in a
December 1964 editorial the question whether it was time to replace
the liquid-fueled rockets of the Atlas and Titan type with solid-fueled
rockets of the Minuteman and Polaris types:

Who decides whether or not the Russians have lost heart sufficiently? The
Kremlin, not us. How many rockets do we need in order to reduce their desire
to attack? That is something for the Soviets to say, and not us. The Secretary
of Defense, McNamara, should know that the hand can be dealt in such a way
that not even four aces are enough to win a poker game. That happens when
your opponent is on to the game you are playing.

But at least it is preferable to have this terrible game of poker played
out in the laboratories of the Rand Corporation or in corresponding
laboratories in Siberia.

—Jacques Bergier

Giants in the Universe: The Quasars

Ceaselessly the endless rolls towards the bottomless.

—Victor Hugo

Beyond the active radiation of our imagination.

—H. P. Lovecraft

A NEW PHYSICS IS BORN

Something happens in the cosmos that exceeds by far everything that the human imagination in science and science fiction has been capable of inventing. Heavenly bodies have been discovered which generate more energy than an entire galaxy and are nevertheless—at least in the opinion of many scientists—hardly larger than an ordinary sun. For the time being, the name quasar, an abbreviation of the English "quasi stellar radio sources," has been given to these objects. They were discovered initially by means of radio astronomy. Then reports came from the observatories on Mount Wilson and Mount Palomar, which have the most powerful optical telescopes, that they too had discovered some quasars.

Later it was discovered that quasars move through the universe at extraordinarily high speed; they attain a velocity of almost 46 per cent the speed of light. Since they emit powerful quantities of energy, they can be observed from much greater distances than a normal solar system.

A galaxy is a grouping of stars into a luminous band extending across the skies of the universe, with a diameter of approximately 50,000 light-years. It is composed of, on the average, 100 billion stars. It is very improbable that all the stars in a single galaxy would explode simultaneously. If they did, they would radiate as much energy as a quasar does.

185

In 1963 quasars were already causing a lot of headaches, but in January 1964 it became much worse. It was established that many quasars had changed their brightness within six months. Now a heavenly body the size of a galaxy cannot possibly change in brightness in so short a space of time, since it takes thousands of years for light to travel from one end of the system to the other. On the other hand, if a quasar is no bigger than an ordinary star and far smaller than a galaxy, how can it possibly emit so much energy?

On May 15, 1964, the scientific-technological newsletter of the American periodical *Technical Science,* in a report on a conference of the American Physical Society, had this to say on quasars:

In the course of the past twelve months radioastronomers have discovered nine "quasars," those huge, glowing, shimmering clouds of gas which are too big for stars and too small to be galaxies. The quasars emit light beams and radio waves from distances up to 10 billion light-years.

At the spring congress of the American Physical Society two physicists presented new facts about the powerful mechanism for the production of energy that must be contained within the quasars. Louis Gold and John W. Moffat from the Institute of Advanced Studies at the Martin Company in Baltimore, Maryland, postulated that in order to be capable of radiating light beams and radio waves as far as the earth, a quasar must produce more energy per second than a quadrillion hydrogen bombs.

There are therefore sources of energy in the universe that are infinitely more powerful than nuclear energy or even the complete destruction of matter, energy sources just as difficult for us to understand as was solar energy for the scholars of the nineteenth century. Since the ambition of the scientists of our time knows no bounds, they try to find explanations. But before we go into these attempts at explanation, which stretch the human imagination to its outermost limits and yet probably do not extend it enough, we should know the basic facts about this extraordinary phenomenon.

WHAT ARE QUASARS?

It is generally assumed that the quasars are extremely distant from us, somewhere between the order of 2 and 10 billion light-years. The quasar 3C273 is said to be 2 billion, the quasar 3C147, 6 to 8 billion light-years away (3C means Third Cambridge Catalogue, *i.e.* the third Cambridge listing of the stars; 273 and 147 are from the continuous numbers in this catalogue).

These distances have been calculated from the fact that the light arriving on the earth from these objects has a red hue, which usually means considerable velocity.

But other explanations are possible. The mass of the quasars may be so dense that the light can escape only with difficulty, and, following the Einstein effect, shifts toward red.

This hypothesis is, however, rejected by most astronomers. And yet it would be possible, as the French scientist Georges Courtes writes in his book on the galaxies, that quasars are extraordinarily dense stars which "man at the present time is not yet able to explain."

If the quasars turn out to be fairly near us, perhaps even within our own Milky Way, then we shall have to revise all our previous notions. In this case the space in which we live must be subject to modifications of a very subtle kind at present completely unknown to us. The July 1964 issue of *The Sciences,* organ of the New York Academy of Sciences, said: "The Einstein equations retain their validity, but it seems now that they are possibly incomplete." In other words: even if the quasars are so dense that they buckle the space around them, preventing their gravitational pull from affecting us, they still must be influencing our space in other subtle ways, bombarding us with elemental particles, without our having as yet any perception of it.

Scientists have come to the realization that we are not living in a Euclidean world but in a space-time continuum. If we now have to come to terms with the idea that the space in which we live is much more complicated than Einstein thought, then the world becomes very disturbing. And so, although decisive proof is still lacking, we want to assume that the quasars are extremely distant from us, and move on to another question.

AS BIG AS A GALAXY OR SMALLER THAN A STAR?

It is obviously possible that quasars are galaxies in which the explosion of a large number of stars is set off by a chain reaction (as in the explosion of an ammunition dump). For reasons not yet within our capabilities of imaginative comprehension, the shock waves of this chain reaction spread faster than the speed of light, which contradicts the Einstein theories. That would explain the variations in brightness, which would otherwise be inexplicable in an object several thousand light-years distant. Many astronomers feel that such a complete upset of physics has to be faced. But most astronomers shy away from the problem, and the reason is not hard to understand. The speed of light represents only a convenient, not an absolute, speed limit—like the sound barrier, for instance. But setting the speed of light as the upper limit is reasonable, considering the structure of matter. An object or signal that exceeds the speed of light would be forced to accelerate into the past, to turn time back.

In a material medium, in which light is braked, no object can be faster than light without breaking the Einsteinian laws. But in a vacuum, journeys into the past and the transmission of signals to the past would be possible. Science fiction authors have taken up this possibility, but for the ordinary mind this hypothesis is unimaginable. And so we prefer to let it drop and share the opinion of the majority of astronomers who see quasars as far-off objects far smaller than the galaxies. The situation is fantastic and exciting enough without throwing out Einstein's theories unnecessarily and hastily, or modifying the space-time continuum through objects of infinite density.

THE THEORY OF HOYLE AND NARLIKAR

What explanations of quasars have been offered that do not depart too radically from traditional science? The theory of Hoyle and Narlikar should be mentioned first.

It is difficult to explain this theory without distorting it. We will have to make use of a few images as we go along. In what follows I lean heavily on an article by John David in the news and information sheet of the British Embassy in Paris.

Professor Hoyle and Dr. J.V. Narlikar have postulated a new theory of gravity.

When a child falls down and bangs his nose he experiences gravity directly. Of all the basic physical forces at work in the universe, gravity is the one most familiar to us. And yet for the scientist it still remains a complete mystery.

Science fiction writers, it is true, create worlds without gravity, but in our real world there exists no possibility of interrupting gravity or of restoring it at will; and the "gravitational charge" of a given mass of matter cannot be changed to make it lighter or heavier.

Gravitation, although mysterious, has all the signs of being a fundamental force, the understanding of which must inevitably lead to a better understanding of the world as a whole. That explains why the bold hypotheses of Hoyle and Narlikar have found such strong echoes.

"How can it be proved?" is the first question scientists put when a new theory is introduced. According to Professor Hoyle, his new theory can be proved, although in practice that would not be advisable, as he says, because to do so it would be necessary to switch off half the stars in the universe.

According to the traditional theory of gravity, such a stellar blackout would not change anything on earth; the sky would simply seem a little darker at night. But if the theory of Hoyle and Narlikar is correct, the switch-off would have colossal consequences: the sun would burn twice as hot, and we on earth would discover that our weight had doubled. The orbit of the earth around the sun would be changed, shrinking the distance between them, and we would all be roasted alive.

These hypotheses underline one essential aspect of the Hoyle-Narlikar theory. Einstein, in his general theory of relativity, looked upon gravity as an essentially local phenomenon. The masses of the sun and the earth create a field of gravity that keeps the earth orbiting the sun. For Einstein this field of gravity was a property of space and time, but its existence at a given place—in the solar system—could not, according to Einstein's theory, be influenced by more distant regions of the universe. And so, if these regions were "switched off," the sun and the earth would not be affected in any way.

MYSTERIOUS GRAVITY

To balance this "field theory," Hoyle and Narlikar have set up a "particle theory," according to which gravity affects all matter simultaneously. If half of all the particles of matter in the universe are eliminated, the gravity effective between the remaining particles is influenced correspondingly.

Only mathematical specialists can follow in detail the arguments that lead to this conclusion. But although the new theory is difficult to understand and to prove, one of its advantages is that it provides explanations that satisfy ordinary common sense, which Einstein's theory does not.

Whereas equations set up by Einstein to explain his theory of gravity would be just as valid in a completely empty universe—imagine a space-time continuum without any kind of matter—in the theory of Hoyle and Narlikar the equations would disappear if matter were to disappear. Gravity—and consequently physics—can only exist when at least two particles are present in the universe and influencing each other. This statement does at least seem to correspond with good human common sense.

Satisfying also to the mind is the idea in the new theory that gravity is equal to the force of attraction—apples fall down, they do not jump up. That is different in Einstein's theory. A mathematician from another world could not tell from Einstein's equations whether gravity in our world represented attraction or repulsion. In the equations themselves it is expressed merely through the signs $+$ or $-$. Mathematically speaking, the choice is arbitrary; Einstein decided to use the minus sign to express the observed fact that gravity is the equivalent of attraction. The theory of Hoyle and Narlikar eliminates this arbitrariness. Their equations show without ambiguity that apples must inevitably fall.

Gravity occupies today a fairly sizable section of science. Its unique quality is that it affects all matter in precisely the same measure, whereas electrical or nuclear phenomena behave differently according to the substances and particles. In addition, gravity is extremely weak compared with electrical or nuclear force. It is perceptible only in gigantic masses, as for instance the earth.

When we fall down, the attraction that the mighty mass of the earth exerts upon our body makes itself felt. But we do not notice the infinitely smaller pull exerted by a mountain or a house—yet it exists.

One of the future tasks of physics will be to work out a theory that takes account of the weakness of gravity and its special properties, and simultaneously aligns it with other physical forces. Such a theory of unity is not in sight yet, but Hoyle and Narlikar believe that it can be achieved.

The new theory postulated by the two scientists can be applied also to certain problems raised by quasars. Strangely enough, before the discovery of quasars Professor Hoyle and the American scientist William Fowler had introduced the hypothesis that in theory giant clouds of gas in the universe could sometimes "implode," that is to say, explode inward. The implosion would cause formations remarkably like the "quasi-stars."

Hoyle and Fowler next studied the processes that normally lead to the formation of a galaxy of stars. A cloud of gas contracts and splits up into a number of small clouds from which the stars originate. The two scientists thought that it could sometimes happen that the cloud did not fall apart. In such an event it would continue to contract under the influence of its own gravity so that the entire mass would collapse with mounting acceleration and energy inward to the center of the gas cloud.

This implosion would lead to a very extraordinary formation, in the center of which would be unimaginably dense matter. A fragment one-thousandth the size of a pinhead would weigh one million tons.

CONSTANTLY SELF-GENERATING WORLDS?

A number of physicists are at work at the present time on the problem of what goes on in the interior of these imploding heavenly bodies. Hoyle and Narlikar are of the opinion that the matter is very possibly completely destroyed and that it disappears into what they call the "field of creation."

According to Hoyle's famous theory, which postulates a constant process of creation in the universe, matter is emerging unceasingly from this field to balance the expansion of the universe observed by the astronomers. For some time now it has been known that the distant galaxies observable by radio telescope are moving away from the earth, some at powerful speeds. Without a constant process of creation the universe would empty itself. According to Hoyle, the average density of matter in the universe remains constant because of the never-ending re-creation of matter. And yet sometimes the very reverse of this process can sometimes observed in the interior of quasars: through the ''sinking'' induced by gravity a certain mass of matter can be directed into the field of creation.

At first these theories might seem strange, but they do seem to correspond to a remarkable degree with all that it has been possible to observe of quasars up to now. It may well be that they also explain the enormous luminous power and the strong radio-wave emission of quasars.

It looks as though these quasi-stars get their energy from gravity, whereas the energy of ordinary stars is generated by nuclear reactions. It must be becoming clear how important the new theories of gravity are.

Hoyle believes that the new astronomical observations and the new theories deduced from them can influence the physics of the earth profoundly. Without doubt we are living through an age of change, and it is thoroughly possible that our world-view will be very different just a few years from now. Men like Hoyle and Narlikar will have contributed a great deal to that transformation.

If quasars are what Hoyle and Narlikar believe they are, then the universe is far more complex and far more subtly organized than has been previously assumed. The universe would then be a mechanism that automatically makes good losses of matter that occur when galaxies exceed the speed of light and disappear, by generating new matter in the interior of the quasars. The quasars may in fact be laboratories in which matter is first generated and then hurled out beyond our universe into an unimaginably gigantic system—into the field of creation.

IS THERE AN ASTRONOMICAL CODE, LIKE THE GENETIC CODE?

According to Hoyle, the matter so created would reappear throughout the entire universe in the form of hydrogen atoms. How are the self-regulating mechanisms structured in a whole so beautifully attuned to its own parts? There is no answer to this question. Albert Ducrocq has put forward the hypothesis that the universe functions like life itself. It is anxious to reduce entropy and have anti-chance win out over chance.

That is a poetic idea which Teilhard de Chardin would certainly have liked.

But when it is examined under the sober light of science a number of questions must be raised. Suppose we have a galaxy with a certain mass of matter that leaves our universe because its velocity exceeds the speed of light. How does the universe "know" that a certain number of quasars must be generated in order to balance out the loss of matter. Where does the "information" come from? How is it transmitted? If the mechanism is self-regulating, how does it function?

If Ducrocq, Hoyle, Narlikar, and also Costa de Beauregard are right, then the universe is just as highly organized and functions just as precisely as a DNA molecule. Just as the genetic code could be discovered, so it must be possible to discover the astronomical code. The information is not limited to living matter, but forms an integral part of the universe, like matter and energy. That would mean a fundamental revision of our ideas. Science has not spoken its last word by a long way.

But we should not forget that the theory of Hoyle and Narlikar does not stand alone. Even if we restrict ourselves to the theories admitting no higher velocity than the speed of light, we still have a choice of a wide variety of theories, one more fantastic than the other. An American, for instance, claimed recently that quasars were ionized masses of gas (plasma) surrounding an immensely dense, unimaginably hot core, comparable to a huge reactor. The particles generated by the fusion speed through the vibrating plasma, radiating resonance and radio waves, which are emitted into the cosmos. Physicists make it clear that the known physical laws, along with laboratory observations of the behavior of plasma, explain to their complete satisfaction the generation and dissemination of the waves. They take into account in their deliberations another factor known as "free Debye energy." This energy, discovered in 1923 by the Dutchman J.W. Debye, was hitherto thought to be too weak to be capable of transforming thermal energy into electromagnetic energy in the form, for instance, of radio waves. But in the context of objects the size of quasars, this energy must represent a quite considerable factor.

This theory has the advantage of seeming to agree with common sense. Its inadequacy lies in the fact that it fails to explain the enormous energy quotient of quasars, unless there are reactions or transformations of matter or energy of a completely unknown kind taking place in the interior of quasars. During these reactions not only nuclear energy but also other energies are at work, possibly a space energy designated by many physicists as subquantum energy.

The American theory in this form was supported by the Soviet astrophysicist Nikolai Kardachev, well-known because of his claim that there must be an intelligent extragalactic culture in the area of the radio star CTA 102. Kardachev defended his view with great emphasis on May 12, 1964, at a conference of the Physics Institute of the Soviet Academy of Sciences. He is of the opinion that magnetic fields compressed in the interior of a thermonuclear superreactor are capable of releasing unsuspected quantities of energy.

Many prominent Soviet academicians, especially Vitali Ginsberg, are skeptical. They prefer to await the results of experiments being conducted at this time before they build any further on the hypothesis.

HOFTMANN'S IDEA:
ANNOYANCE AS THE ANTI-MATTER

Banesh Hoftmann is a distinguished American physicist who teaches at Columbia University and who was one of Einstein's collaborators. He supports the theory of the existence of paranormal phenomena and was one of the first to observe that there are physical agencies, the neutrino for instance, that travel through all impediments and could well be the intermediaries of parapsychological phenomena.

It was necessary that a man of his culture and imagination postulate an original theory about the quasars. It was published in the May 1965 issue of the excellent English periodical *Science Journal*.

Hoftmann's fundamental thesis is often found in science fiction, but not in scientific publications. The thesis is that there is such a thing as negative matter. Not anti-matter, which is matter with a charge opposite to that of ordinary matter, but rather matter with a negative mass, which is to say, neutral particles or particles with a mass smaller than zero charged positively or negatively. Such matter would be repulsed by ordinary matter. It would possess an anti-gravitational force and a negative inertia. In science fiction novels interstellar spaceships are often powered by such matter.

Science fiction authors can allow themselves liberties; scientists must be more cautious. But Hoftmann throws caution to the winds and demonstrates with great brilliance that negative matter, if it exists, must generate veritable hurricanes of energy by acting on ordinary matter, leading to the genesis of quasars. A negative particle has not so far been discovered by anyone, but that does not discourage Hoftmann. After all, Dirac predicted the existence of anti-matter before it was actually discovered.

It is true that negative matter would explain the existence of quasars, but its own existence has not yet been proved by either astronomical observation or laboratory experiments. The question is justified as to whether it makes sense to explain one mystery by another.

I myself believe that the problem of quasars must be approached with an open mind. The possibility has to be admitted that we have here something completely new that transcends our knowledge and our imagination. We are in approximately the same position as the physicists of the nineteenth century were when they were faced with the problem of solar energy. They realized perfectly well that the sources of energy known to them—chemical combustion, gravitation——could not explain solar energy. And since atomic nuclei and nuclear energy were still unknown to them, it was impossible for them to postulate hypotheses capable of elucidating solar energy properly and correctly.

Quasars present us with a similar problem. A completely new source of energy, which at the present time cannot be explained, generates these giants of the universe.

—Jacques Bergier

Unsuspected Possibilities

When man's fantasy began to dwell on the possibilities his own brain, it first focused on the surgeon and his miracle-working scalpel, dreaming of operations to afford man unlimited capabilities. Arthur Machen, in his novella *The Great God Pan,* describes an operation that opens the portals of perception so wide that all the forces of nature are revealed to the patient.

Others have dreamed of the union of the two halves of the brain, by which the memory, the intelligence, and other spiritual capabilities are at least doubled. This experiment has in fact already been carried out on apes, but up to now without any results worthy of note. Science fiction author John W. Campbell predicted the possibility of such operations some thirty years before the scientists began to occupy themselves with this hypothesis.

Some scientists suggest the possibility of brain-transplantation between living organisms of the same or neighboring species. There are, however, still limitations on organ transplantation between humans. As a rule, one organism will reject tissue from another organism, even from a living organism of the same species; only in the case of monovular twins or a mother and daughter does the immunity reaction of the organism fail to set in. But this fundamental difficulty has not inhibited novelists from creating their fantasies.

One of these fantasies comes fairly close to what is possible in fact: a brain is kept alive in a specially prepared culture medium in a jar (the brain of an ape was in fact successfully kept alive in this way for twenty-four hours). This is the theme of Curt Siodmak's novel *Donovan's Brain.* Quite a few other science fiction authors have taken up this possibility. If the brain were washed over in the jar by fresh blood and the waste materials removed, it would theoretically be possible to keep it alive for an unlimited time. And if the brain were equipped with sense organs and connected up with a superefficient electronic brain, it could probably be actively, even if hardly pleasantly, alive. A brain living in a test tube liberated from bodily inconveniences could perhaps learn to make use of the 90 per cent of neurons that according to the estimates of neurologists are lying fallow at any given moment. The brain would also have to have the power to end its life when it grew tired of its state and its prison. This could be done by the transmission of an appropriate electronic signal. The experiment is more like a nightmare than a dream, but it is at any rate an almost realizable dream. A brain isolated in this way would probably not remain human for long, for consciousness, when you think about it, is more than just a function.

JOINING BRAINS MAKES IT POSSIBLE TO LEAD SEVERAL LIVES

It would also be conceivable to transplant onto such a brain additional organs capable of receiving infrared rays, radio waves, X-ray beams, neutrons, and so on. Such organ implantation would almost certainly lead to the development of new, quite remarkable senses.

Still more exciting would be the possibility of recording sensations emitted by the brain on magnetic tape and communicating them to another brain. This process would enable an individual to lead several lives that would not differ in any respect from his own. Science-fiction authors, especially Arthur C. Clarke, have already used this idea extensively. It is worthy of a moment's attention. It would not be wise to misuse a magnetic machine that registered sensations, just as it would not be wise to spend one's entire life at the movies without food or drink. But that is the only reservation. Why should we not lead a multiplicity of lives, why not have a new life every night? The telescope perspective on time that characterizes certain dreams makes this possibility seem thoroughly plausible. The individual could then choose what sort of life he wanted to lead. He could influence his other lives to a certain extent with the help of the reflex curves of the brain recorded on the magnetic tape. Currents emitted by the brain would change the notation correspondingly, which process would grant the individual, as in "real" life, a certain freedom. Such authors as Clifford Simal and Stanislas Lem have used this idea with great inventiveness.

Such fantasies raise serious, even terrible, philosophical questions. How do we know that we ourselves are not just brains sealed into a test tube receiving sensations from some registering machine? Lem comes to the conclusion that the parapsychological phenomena investigated by the narrator of his story are to be explained by deficiencies in the registering machine: telepathy is possible when two magnetic tapes serving different brains are short-circuited, prediction of the future when the tape is incorrectly spooled and messages are transmitted to the brain which should only have come two hours or days or years later. Such a line of argument is hard to disprove. Our reality is after all closely tied in with the brain as it is at present. We possess no scientific proof for the existence of an immortal soul. And without such proof Lem's materialistic nightmare is not unreasonable.

MIND-CONTROLLED MACHINES

Science has already succeeded in coupling brain and machine to a certain extent. In the Soviet Union disabled persons have been provided with mind-controlled artificial limbs. When the handicapped person wants to clench his fist, electric currents flow into the wrist to activate the hand muscles. In the event that the disabled person has lost his hand in consequence of an accident or a wound, the current is increased to drive tiny electronic motors, which move the artificial hand.

On the basis of this accomplishment it would be possible to imagine—as has indeed been done in many futuristic novels—mind-controlled airplanes or spaceships. A mind-controlled aircraft would have many advantages in warfare. However, in a spaceship traveling at 6 miles per second, the nerve currents would be transmitted too slowly; it is therefore preferable in such cases to use fully automated electronic devices, since electrons can travel virtually at the speed of light.

But the possibilities of the future are not limited to the scalpel and to connecting the brain to electronic mechanisms. Drugs, both known and unknown, open up a still wider vista. The classic book on this subject is Robert Louis Stevenson's *Dr. Jekyll and Mr. Hyde,* the one and only detective story in which the solution of the mystery is more horrible than the mystery itself. Arthur Machen too dealt with the effect of drugs in a tragic tale called *The White Powder.* It is the story of an unfortunate apothecary who had a very complex, compound medicine that changes into a witches' Sabbath potion as a consequence of an extremely rare chemical reaction. Wells dreamed of drugs in *The New Accelerator,* a thought-provoking short story containing in particular a treatise on the significance of the organic phosphates—fifty years before science occupied itself with the subject. In *The Hound of Tindalos* John Belknap Smith describes the exploration of time through the use of a drug.

Endless dreams are possible about drugs. It would be nice to have drugs that dull pains without blunting the sensitivities of the organism. Effective aphrodisiacs are searched for in vain, and one wonders if they exist only in legends and advertisements. The majority of recipes of this type to be found in the literature of magic are dangerous or useless.

DO DRUGS MAKE BETTER PEOPLE?

The greatest dream of all is for a drug that would make people better. That is not altogether just a silly thought. Serious scientists are occupying themselves with the idea, among them Henri Laborit, in his essay in *La Presse Medicale* of March 27, 1965:

It may well be that pharmacology will play a prominent role in the future evolution of mankind. Many naturalists, many lovable old men and people who still yearn for the ''good old days'' and who want to ''return to Mother Nature,'' will reply that pharmacology is not ''natural.'' But what is natural? Either everything is natural or nothing is natural. When man made fire or tore off a fig leaf to cover his shame his behavior no longer corresponded to the purity of nature as our opponents understand it. As soon as a value judgment is introduced into a human action it is important to bear in mind that this happens because of an arbitrary decision and that we are conditioned phylogenetically, genetically, and semantically to make value judgments. I do not see why it should be more forbidden to man, at the moment when he becomes aware of his place in the evolutionary process of nature, to adjust those aspects of his behavior which still contain animal elements, than it should be forbidden him to invent the automobile, for which nobody reproaches him. All in all man, who has modified his environment profoundly, still possesses in the twentieth century the brain of his cave-dwelling ancestors. This brain has remained biologically the same, and has become heavier only through a semantic apparatus handed down carefully from generation to generation for the protection of the social structures, which are themselves for the most part outdated.

The shortest route to the removal of this dangerous state of affairs seems to us perhaps—I say "perhaps" intentionally—to use pharmacological medicines to eliminate the functioning, in most cases no longer adequate functioning, of this paleolithic brain; man has lugged this brain around with him through the centuries, while managing to replace his hands by machines, his feet by much faster methods of transportation, to improve his eyes by optical or electronic systems. At the same time he found it totally natural to penetrate certain secrets of the regulation of matter. And finally I do not believe that mankind distorts the will of that man who came to us two thousand years ago to preach peace on earth, if he takes this step on the day—perhaps not far distant—when it becomes possible for him.

The scientist who made this statement is experimenting with such drugs and has already had some results. A whole series of substances would be conceivable for each stated purpose, for example, a drug to calm violent mentally disturbed patients. Laborit seems to have found such a drug already.

There would also be a drug to rehabilitate criminals. Several variations of this drug are possible:

A drug might conceivably be used to extinguish from the mind everything stored there during imprisonment. The criminal could be given a course to reeducate him for society.

A drug could also make criminals especially receptive to hypnotic suggestion. Through posthypnotic influence it could perhaps be possible to persuade them not to commit a crime again.

Another drug would genuinely rehabilitate the criminal by restoring his inner equilibrium and so controlling certain secretions which seem to be responsible for his criminal tendencies.

WILL PSYCHOCHEMISTRY CONQUER MODERN MAN'S FEAR OF LIFE?

There is obviously no point in arguing whether it is possible to extinguish original sin or human free will with the aid of the right

chemical molecule. Not everyone believes in original sin. And so far
as free will is concerned, this free will is far more inhibited when one
has a terrible toothache than when one eases the pain with the proper
drug. It is equally conceivable that the criminal has more free will
when certain instincts are strongly repressed. It should be noted further
that psychotherapeutic treatment, using the appropriate drugs, restricts
the will far less than does, for instance, prison or the house of
detention.

Continuing the dream, one arrives at drugs that would relax drivers
and reduce violence in everyday life. Demonstrators could be brought
around to reason at the very climax of their rage by means of a gaseous
substance sprayed at them. Drugs have even been thought of that were
intended to pacify a whole army. One could also think of drugs capable
of taming the wildest of animals. Such drugs could be applied as a
spray or in the form of a smoke bomb. If this dream seems fantastic, let
it be remembered that there are microbes, much more dangerous than
any tiger, which have been rendered harmless by pharmaceutical
chemistry.

Finally, one could imagine modern man's fear of life being removed
by drugs. Fear is a phenomenon of which the causes are not well
known. Many fears are conscious, others unconscious. It looks as
though certain unmotivated fears not capable of being relieved by
psychotherapeutic treatment might be of chemical origin. If this is
correct, it should be possible to find a chemical antidote. There is no
lack of patients on whom to try out the drugs. An estimated 15 per cent
of adults in industrial nations suffer from severe anxiety neuroses.
Many of them would come forward voluntarily if doctors were to begin
with the testing of a new drug against fear. Therefore the research
merits an intensification.

INTELLIGENCE PILLS?

Man has often dreamed of drugs that would increase intelligence. In
spite of all the criticisms that can be leveled at human intelligence, it
remains a very useful thing. It is supposed to be "rounded off" by
emotion and supported by intuition, but for survival and success it is a

very important factor. In laboratory experiments the level of intelligence of animals has already been successfully raised with the help of drugs. The experiments have been carefully verified. Unfortunately the drugs used for the purpose have also been very poisonous. A good example is nicotine. Animals injected with a strong dose of nicotine become noticeably more intelligent, but die quickly.

Nevertheless, a drug may be found that would raise the intelligence through nicotine yet at the same time not be poisonous. Several questions suggest themselves:

Would such a drug bring about a leveling, so that all men were equal in intelligence?

Or would the effect of the drug be that stupid men would become intelligent and intelligent men geniuses?

At what age would this drug have to be taken?

Would you have to keep taking it in order to avoid an unpleasant relapse, like the one described by Daniel Keyes in *Flowers for Algernon*?

Are there—apart from possible mutations—limits to human intelligence?

These are questions to which there are no answers but which provide the stimulus for continued dreams. On the social plane an aristocracy could be imagined that reserved the drug for its own use, or a democracy under which the drug would be available to everyone. Would there exist a right to forbid dissemination of the drug? Would an individual be free to refuse to take the drug in order to remain stupid and happy? That would be in my opinion a good subject for a science fiction author. Perhaps the blockheads will inherit the earth, after the superintelligences have finished each other off with death rays and cobalt bombs.

DRUGS REMOVE SPACE AND TIME

Finally, one can leave the safe ground of psychochemistry and indulge in dreams of completely fantastic drugs. Many authors, Aldous Huxley for instance, have said that man could gain happiness through some appropriate substance without ever having really earned it. The English writer John Brunner, in *Put Down This Earth,* invented a drug that transplants the user to a real paradise, to a second earth existing alongside ours but not yet polluted by man and radioactive fallout. According to Brunner, there exist an endless number of such earths, so that every one of us could turn our backs on this planet once and for all to lead a rustic life with a few friends far from nuclear weapons and bugging devices. Drugs are also conceivable that would be capable of awakening telepathic receptivities. The few remaining primitive peoples seem to know about such drugs. It would, however, be necessary to dream up some antidote drug, because telepathic capabilities could be dangerous. Science fiction authors usually have these kinds of drug affect the pincal gland, which since Descartes has been regarded as the seat of the soul. It is at any rate conceivable that this part of the brain corresponds to the so-called psionic capabilities: telepathy, soothsaying, bilocation, predicting the future, telekinetics, and so on.

PERHAPS ELECTRONIC COMPUTERS WILL SOLVE THESE PROBLEMS

If the memory is allied to proteins, as is assumed, these psionic capabilities are perhaps similarly allied; the drugs necessary for their stimulation could therefore be analogous to insulin, a protein skeleton that also bears active molecules. Just as it was possible to analyze insulin and manufacture it synthetically, so it must be possible to work out the formulas of the new drugs by means of data-processing machines.

I do not envy the scientists of the future who take on this task. A rat injected with a drug that permitted it to see into the would probably not behave very peacefully! Experiments with people could lead to all the paradoxes of space and time that the brilliant American science fiction author Alfred Pester has described in *Last Stop: The Stars.* A laboratory in which the volunteers for the experiments and even the scientists themselves begin to travel around without gravity in space and time, where objects move about telekinetically, and where the results of experiments can be altered by sheer will power, would in all probability not be an especially pleasant place. At that time man will begin to sigh for the good old days when science was still uncomplicated and magic had still not been rediscovered.

—Jacques Bergier

The Miracle of the Cell

A JOURNEY TO THE LIMITS OF OUR KNOWLEDGE

A poetic but scientifically accurate image of the cell, drawn according to what biologists know today, could represent it as a planet consisting of totally programmed matter and orbited by satellites on which there were factories. These factories are the ribosomes. The central planet is the nucleus of the cell. Instructions are passed by RNA from the nucleus to the ribosomes. These events make endless speculations possible. It would be possible to "reprogram" the cell nucleus, or alter the ribosomes, or influence the acid as it is transmitting the information.

As far as the nucleus of the cell is concerned, it would be possible—and the possibility has already been weighed—to wipe out the original programming and reprogram it completely from scratch, as can be done with magnetic tape. Several pieces of research, albeit of an extremely controversial nature, permit the surmise that such a dream-fantasy is perhaps not completely absurd. The nucleic acids seem in fact to possess magnetic properties. With a sufficiently sensitive apparatus it might be possible to demagnetize them and then to remagnetize them. In this way it would be possible for instance to alter cancerous cells and to reprogram them to correspond to normal cells.

Of course a cell could only be artificially programmed after man has progressed to reasonably exact knowledge of the genetic code and has developed magnetic instruments of appropriate sensitivity. We are not that far ahead yet. Electrodes fine enough to be introduced into a cell represent biology's present furthest point of progress. It is not far enough, but it is a beginning.

Possible perhaps would be a less ambitious operation consisting of injecting into a cell chemical substances which would change the genetic code. Such experiments have already been carried out on bacteria. It is therefore possible to predict that at some point in the future information will be transmitted to the nucleus and the natural programming will thereby be changed.

Jack Williamson in his book *Dragons' Teeth* solved the problem in a way only science-fiction authors can allow themselves: he describes a telekinetic influencing of the cell nucleus. Williamson exhausts all the possibilities of an idea that is clearly as absurd as all science-fiction ideas—until they are realized.

PROGRAMMED CELLS PRODUCE ANY DESIRED SUBSTANCE AND EFFECT MUTATIONS

If man were successful, by paramagnetic induction, by chemical or by other methods, in altering the orders transmitted to the ribosomes in a cell, it would be possible to raise bacteria that produce aspirin, to isolate rare metals from seawater, or even to transform one metal into another. The ribosomes themselves could be used as culture mediums that would represent far more efficient chemical factories than even the most perfect one created by human hands: factories to create crude oil from gases or sugar and fats from air, all at normal temperatures and normal pressures, that is to say in the most economical way possible.

Scientists have hitherto not occupied themselves to any great extent with the possibility of influencing RNA. Nevertheless, new experiments do give reason for further thought. It might be possible to remove the RNA from a cell, transform it, then inject it into another cell. In this way cancer-fighting cultures could be cultivated that destroy a cancerous growth and then themselves disintegrate.

The experiments carried out by Mituru Tanakami at the University of California in Berkeley have shown that it is possible to isolate from the ribosomes the protein molecule chains supplied by RNA. The process is one of extremely complex "chemical surgery." A ribosome is tiny, only about one hundred Ångstrom units in length (one-tenth of a millimeter). And yet this miniature organism resembles a factory, and along its surface proteins are rendered polymeric (polymerization=compounding to macromolecules). RNA is a chain of about 80 amino acid molecules. It approaches the ribosomes and orders them to form a certain kind of protein molecule. This mechanism is as miraculous as it is precise. It is responsible for the fact that children resemble their parents and that a rose can never beget a cat.

In principle the process is not all too different from the transmission—by mail or special messenger—of a program set up in Paris to a data-processing machine situated, say, in Marseille. In practice it is a far more complex matter, but research like that of Mituru Tanakami raises hopes that RNA can perhaps be altered on its way from the cell nucleus to the ribosome. Such a possibility would provide much free play to the imagination. Anticancerous RNA could be provided over wide areas, a foetus could be injected with a serum or a synthetic virus that would lead to the formation of a brain surpassing anything hitherto known. A distinguished scientist at the Pasteur Institute said recently that a development along these lines was not impossible. The "superman" would then be created not by a mutation of man but by influencing the embryo. If one dares to mention such possibilities at public lectures the general reaction is: "They'll never dare try that!" But man has always been daring, and this time he will no doubt be willing to venture again.

ELECTRONIC BRAINS OUT OF LIVING MATTER?

Let us turn now to another controversial issue. Memory banks for data-processing machines consisting of RNA can be imagined. Somehow the information to be transmitted to a ribosome would be offloaded onto RNA. The information on the ribosome would be "read off" by a detector—a receiver developed to a high level of perfection working with infrared. An apparatus of this kind would be the ultimate in data-processing installations. A highly sophisticated electronic computer could then be fitted into a briefcase. In the place of extremely expensive crystals, ribosomes taken from cells or more simple microbes would be used, which could be cultivated on any organic waste materials. Replacing the huge, expensive, more and more strongly centralized machines would be relatively small electronic-bio-logical instruments which use only small amounts of energy and are cheap enough to be within the range of everyone's budget. One gram of RNA seems to contain about one billion times more information than one gram of the best ferrite (at the present time ferrite is generally used for the storage apparatus of data-processing machines). Such a "live" computer would of course have to be protected from infection, but that would hardly raise problems more difficult than those presented by the data-processing machines in use today. The rooms in which the machines are kept are as sterile as an operating room. Why not then computers based on living matter?

COLOR TELEVISION PICTURES
WITH INDUSTRIALLY PRODUCED MICROBES

It is as yet difficult to see how a receiver could be installed on a ribosome; miniaturization has limits that RNA has probably reached. But data-processing machines would not of course be the only kinds of instruments that could benefit from a biologically constructed information storage plant.

The process could have significance for color television. One has only to think of the gigantic quantities of magnetic tape necessary for the recording of television programs to realize the simply endless commercial possibilities that open up on this front alone. In theory the matter is simple. Microbes would have to be cultivated, crushed, centrifugalized to isolate the genetic components like the nucleic acids, the programming wiped out, and new electronic impulses recorded, which then could be played back.

Following up this principle, it would be possible to conceive of a manufacturing installation in the future at which the raw material consists of cultured bacteria. The bacteria are pulped with the aid of ultra-sound, the nucleic acids decentrifugalized and processed to a filament which is then passed through an X-ray field and neutralized. Color television programs are then recorded on the nucleic acid filaments, and played back by running the filaments through an appropriate takeoff spool.

But let us return to the whole cell. First we will consider the membrane that isolates the interior from the outside world. Today billions are invested in the effort to re-create such membranes.

Obviously it is not composed simply of matter but also of forces that form a kind of barricade. If man is one day capable of reproducing such a membrane artificially, he will be able to convert seawater into drinking water at virtually no cost and in addition generate electricity. A wonderful dream, but to realize it knowledge is necessary about what the mysterious force is that is set into motion in the cell membrane. At the moment the surmise is that the force is of electrostatic or osmotic nature. Electrostatic forces are a phenomenon known to us. Hardly anything more is known about the osmotic force than is known about its effects. In contradiction to the laws of gravity this force causes the juices in plants to rise to sometimes scarcely believable levels.

WILL THE CELL REVEAL TO US THE SECRET OF PHYSICAL IMMORTALITY?

At the Brooklyn Polytechnic Institute Professor Weiss pulps a hen feather so completely that even the cells are smashed. The mass is then introduced into a suitable culture medium. The cells re-form themselves and construct a new hen feather. In the case of many animals such processes are automatic. We are therefore justified in dreaming of dissolving man in cells and re-forming him after expurgation of the poisons. That is the fountain of youth, the blood baths of the secret cults like the Magna Mater.

AMOEBAS AS BIG AS OXEN

How big can the cell become once gravity is eliminated and biology is able to provide it with unlimited growth? This question has been a popular one since the formulation of the plan to establish laboratories on space stations. It would be of immense value to possess cancerous cells of huge dimensions, because they could then be much more effectively researched. It would also be interesting to know the size attainable by single-celled creatures, the amoeba for instance, if gravity were eliminated and they were allowed to grow without interference. The near future might very well make such experiments a possibility. Science fiction already has tales of giant amoebas that have escaped from the laboratory of some mad scientist.

Something of that kind is impossible on earth, since gravity would force such a monster onto the ground. But it would be possible in the cosmos, or to be more precise, in a laboratory hanging in space and surrounded by its own atmosphere. Does space have single- or multiple-celled living organisms? Perhaps. It is still not known what the fireflies were that Glenn and Titov observed in space. The official explanation that they were "bits of paint coming off from the cabin of a spaceship" does not make sense when the fierce heat to which the space capsule is exposed on the launching pad is considered. The temperature at launching is far higher than any temperatures when the ship is in orbit, yet no particles of paint detached themselves then. In their novel *Tales of Outer Space* the American science-fiction authors Jack Williamson and Frederic Pohl work on the premise that animals can live in space. That is a nice dream, but whether it can become fact is still not known.

CELLS AS MASTERS OF ESPIONAGE

Much thought has been given to the possibility of picking up rays emitted by the cell, especially during the splitting of the cell. The American biologist George Crile claims to have discovered phosporescent spots of high temperature in the interior of the cell, and has called them "radio genes." No other scientist has been able to detect these "radio genes." They would however be very useful in helping to explain the transmutation phenomena that our friend Kervan believed he had proved.

If the "radio genes" exist in fact, then the cell would have to emit ultraviolet radiations from time to time. Many scientists, among them the Russian Vurvitch, are of the opinion that they have tracked down such radiations, and call them "mitogenetic rays."

While working in the laboratory of Prof. René Audubert I had an unfortunate experience. We were in the process of testing an especially sensitive detector, a so-called photon-counter. (This is a Geiger counter in which one electrode is sensitized with iodine.) Our instrument picked up everything, including mitogenetic rays. Its sensitivity ranged from visible blue light to cosmic rays. Biologists brought all kinds of cells to us, and we discovered the most surprising rays. Already I was harboring hopes that the work would yield for me one of those dissertations that turn out to be a milestone in a scientist's life and epoch-making for the world of science as a whole. Then I hit upon the fateful idea of grounding both the photon-counter and the ray-emitting agencies. The phenomenon disappeared immediately, and I have never been able to detect the radiations again. Other scientists have had just as little success. Until today the existence of radiations emanating from the cell remains unproven. It seems not to emit radiation either when stationary or during cell division. It would be nice if the cell were to emit radiation that would tell us whether it is healthy, so that its equilibrium could if necessary be restored. But that is likely to remain just a dream in our time.

The theme of cells that emit rays has been used by many science-fiction authors, in excellent novels, for instance the Russian writer Dolguchin and the American Robert Heinlein. Heinlein even offered a "scientific" explanation for his rays. He starts from the premise that apart from the spectrum of electromagnetic waves, which we are slowly learning to deal with, there exist three other radiation spectrums: one that is gravitational-magnetic, one gravitational-electric, and one three-phased gravitational-electromagnetic spectrum. In this way he is able to explain rays of a completely new kind. In dreams and in science fiction the premise is legitimate that the functioning cell emits rays corresponding to its genetic code.

Accordingly the Frenchman Jacques Spitz invents in his book *Cell Z* a cell isolated from its human organism that is placed between two panes of glass in a shallow layer of fluid. A field of force is used to compel it to imitate the movements of the organism from which it comes. All that would be necessary to create the most perfect and successful espionage instrument in history would be to trace a map on the glass pane. But one day the man from whom the cell was taken dies; yet the cell in the fluid continues to move. Is it controlled by something left behind by the dead man? Or are the movements purely reflex movements? Wisely enough the author leaves the answers to these questions to the reader.

RESTORATION OF A LIVING ORGANISM FROM A SINGLE CELL

The possibility has been pondered of reproducing an entire organism from a single cell by increasing the strength of the radiations emanating from the cell and directing them into a neutral, malleable solution of organic matter. This is the fundamental notion underlying the stories of George F. Worts in *The Return of George Washington* and of Maurice Renard and Albert Jean in *The Ape*. There are in addition at least fifty to a hundred science-fiction novels on this subject but the two books named offer the richest fare to the imagination. A serious work on the same subject is Arthur C. Clarke's *Profile of the Future*. The Polish writer Stanislaus Lem devoted an essay to the question, which was published in the Belgian periodical *Techniques Nouvelles*.

The idea seems ghoulish at first: if you can "reproduce" Mr. Smith simply from a cell of one of his hairs, then who is the real Mr. Smith? And a still knottier question: If George Washington could be reproduced from a few of the cells which remained alive in his dead body, what would the effect of his reappearance be on our present-day world? Clarke and Lem, both confirmed materialists, look forward serenely to such a possibility. Maurice Renard and Albert Jean on the other hand introduce into their tales religious feelings and the concept of sinning against the spirit. For them the inventor of methods to reproduce living organisms is no Prometheus but simply the "ape of God."

Like everything that bears on the concept of personal identity this idea of reproduction from a single cell is profoundly disturbing. It would be desirable for this possibility to remain the permanent and exclusive property of science-fiction authors. But will it? While working with carrots and tobacco plants, Frederick C. Stewart of Cornell University succeeded in cultivating normal plants from single cells. Dr. Stewart refuses even to consider the application of the results of his work to mankind, but some of his colleagues do not have the same inhibitions.

It is at any rate certain that every cell nucleus of every single one of our cells—not only the nuclei of our sex cells—contains everything theoretically necessary for our reproduction. The way to actual reproduction through such cells is, however, a long way off.

Let us turn now to a less disturbing subject. If the biologist were successful in discovering the cellular radiations and in deciphering the genetic code of a cell, he would have at his disposal an infallible method of identification. Fingerprints can be altered, but not the genetic code of a cell. It is possible that passport authorities will one day request submission of sample cells with applications for passports or identity cards, so that the genetic code can be recorded.

Once the laws governing the inheriting of the genetic code are known, paternity suits can be brought to a clear and definitive solution by examining the cell nuclei of mother, child, and supposed father. The genetics of today permits only probability judgments. At the same time extreme caution is advisable vis-à-vis the laws of genetics.

IS THE SECRET OF EVOLUTION HIDDEN IN THE CELL?

Science-fiction authors have dreamed of the possibility of generating artificially specialized cells in the embryo after comception that would grow to be specialized organs. A manipulation of this type would be effected by microsurgery or radiations. The American Norman F. Knight has occupied himself with this theme and invented races evolved from man but capable of living in the sea or on other planets. The question here is not one of artificially induced mutations but of a kind of supersurgery surpassing anything possible today. If one considers the monstrous living organisms that Prof. Étienne Wolff has created in the laboratory, then it is not hard to be convinced that the novels of Norman F. Knight are perhaps not quite so absurd as they appear at first sight. There is today the additional factor to be taken into account that surgery is in fact now in a position to operate in the interior of a cell, not with surgical instruments but with the laser beam. Such operations have already been carried out in the laboratory of Professor Bessis in the Centre de Transformation Sanguine in Paris.

Experiments like this one open up wide horizons to the imagination. Working under a supermicroscope, and perhaps also an X-ray microscope, employing the laser beam like a surgical knife, a multiplicity of incisions into the cell should be possible. Strips could be shaved off from the nucleus; the membrane could even be punctured to introduce electrodes or receivers for the extraction of information from the cell. It may also be that the organizational field which determines the movements of the particles in the cell will respond to corresponding instruments. Even just a short time ago the very thought of electrodes smaller than a cell nucleus would have seemed mad. But the technology of integrated circuits brings about the successful peeling off of crystalline layers so tiny that they can be introduced into a cell, where they will perhaps pick up information. For like every living organism, a cell consists not only of matter and energy but also of information. The cell is surrounded by an aura of information, by a biological field of unity, an organizing field, about which we know hardly anything at present. Perhaps this field is the thing we now call "aura." I have never yet seen any registering instrument capable of recording this aura, but I do know sensitive men who claim to be able to perceive it. This field is certainly connected with time. Living organisms evolve because the laws governing the combinations between the various cells change with time. Heredity and natural selection are two manifestations of this evolution, but they are nothing more than manifestations. It is still not known what actually causes evolution. There is not even certainty about whether the cause of evolution is biological. Perhaps there exists a space-time evolutionary field in which the cells deflect in the same way as the needle of a magnet deflects toward the north pole in the magnetic field. It is possible that research in this area will lead to the discovery of this field. For instance, cells could be combined with drops of an electrically charged fluid, and the charged cells then accelerated almost to the speed of light. The effects of the field and the effects of the shifting of time dimensions on the cells could be observed simultaneously. There are no limits to such dreams—even the wildest dreams are permissible.

—Jacques Bergier